Oar & Sail

W9-ADE-825

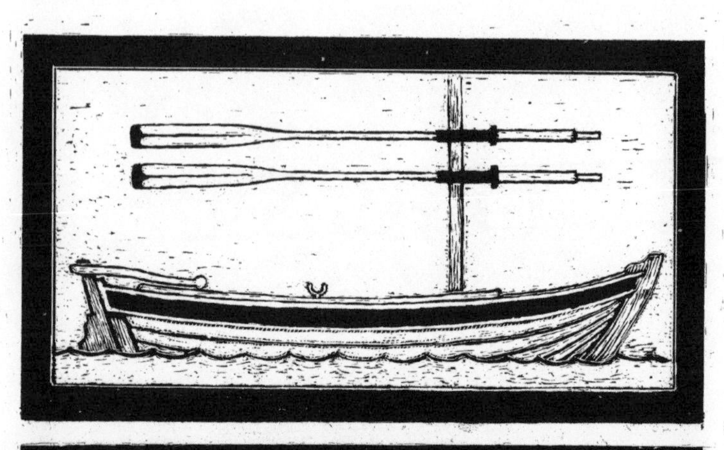

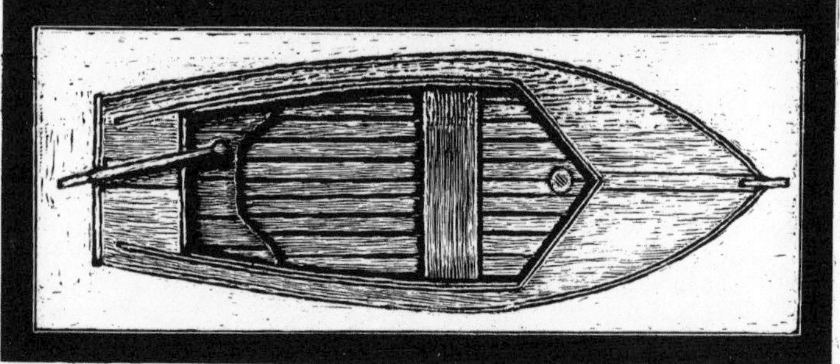

morag anne

Oar & Sail

An Odyssey of the West Coast

Kenneth Macrae Leighton

Illustrations: Roderick Leighton

Creekstone Press Ltd
Smithers, BC
Canada
1999

Copyright © 1999 Nancy and Roderick Leighton
Illustration copyright © 1999 Roderick Leighton

Canadian Cataloguing in Publication Data

Leighton, Kenneth Macrae, 1925-1998
Oar and sail: an odyssey of the west coast

ISBN 0-9684043-1-6 (bound) – ISBN 0-9684043-2-4 (pbk.)
1. Leighton, Ken, 1925-1998 – Journeys – Inside Passage.
2. Morag Anne (Boat) 3. Inside Passage – Description and travel.
4. Boats and boating – Inside Passage. I. Leighton, Rod. II. Title.
FC3845.I5L44 1999 917.11'1 C99-910788-7
F1089.I5L44 1999

All rights reserved.
No part of this work may be reproduced or used in any form or by any means – graphic, electronic or mechanical – without the prior written permission of the publisher.
Requests may be directed to: Creekstone Press Ltd.,
RR #2, S-55, C-2, Smithers, BC V0J 2N0 Canada

Design: Megan Hobson, Jeanie Elsner, Anne Maclean
Illustrations: Roderick Leighton
Layout, maps: Anne Maclean

Printed and bound in Canada

Third Printing: July, 2000

For Bernard,
Morgan, Thomas
and Kirsten

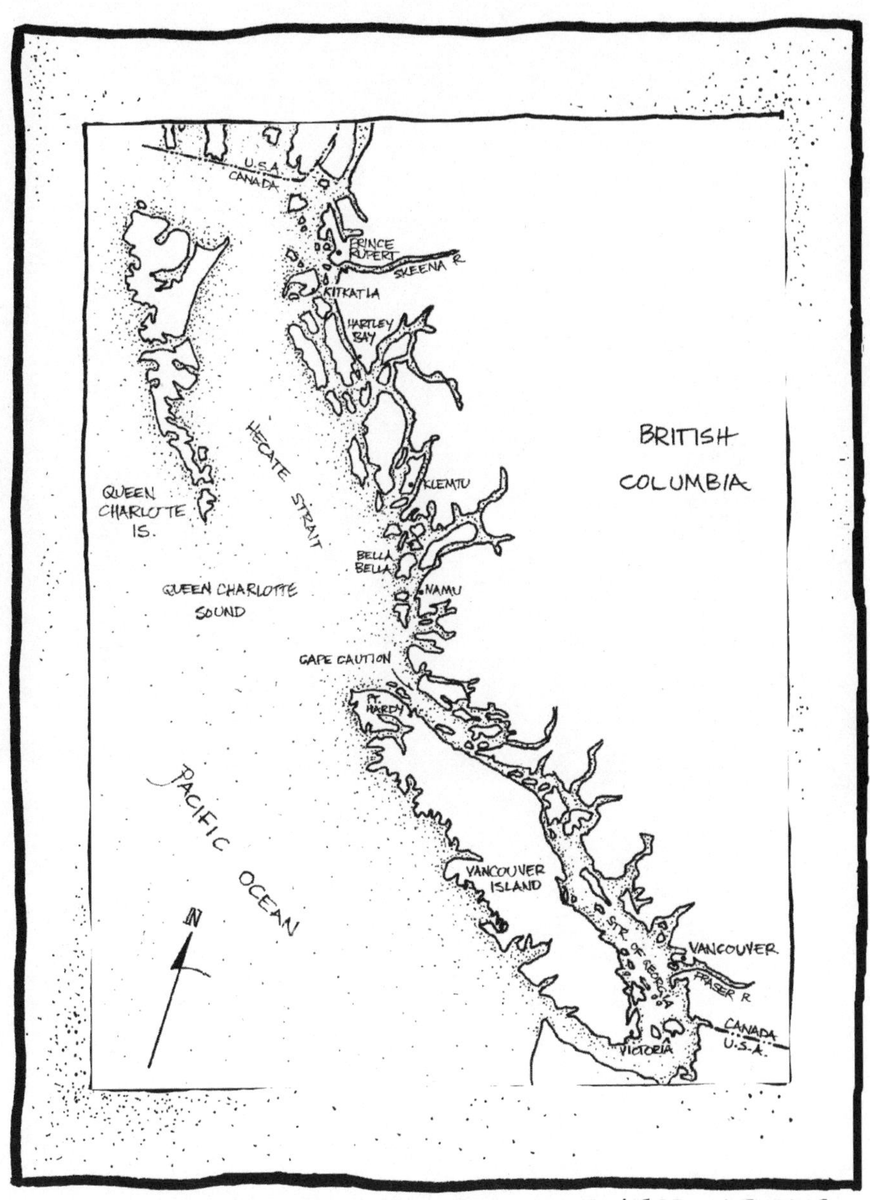

THIS MAP AND FOLLOWING MAPS IN THE BOOK ARE NOT DRAWN TO SCALE.

Foreword

For many, the physical challenge of outdoor adventure is irresistible, especially when combined with foreign travel. Autobiographical accounts by Wilfred Thesiger, Bill Tillman and the Smeetons come to mind and it is not surprising the stories of their exploits were among the favourites of Dr. Kenneth Leighton.

I first met Ken on a rainy, January day in 1952 on the dock at Alert Bay, British Columbia. I was serving as ship's doctor on the Anglican Coast Mission ship, *Columbia II*, and Ken was assisting the legendary flying doctor of Alert Bay, Jack Pickup. Both Ken and I were recent medical school graduates from Aberdeen and Belfast. We hit it off immediately and remained firm friends until his untimely death in 1998.

Ken was born in 1925 in Barbados, British West Indies, but spent all his young, growing years in Scotland, mostly in the area of Crieff, west of Perth. He took his medical training at Aberdeen University and worked for the Royal Army Medical Corps in the Middle East for two years before opening a family practice back in Scotland on the Outer Hebrides.

Ken's adventurous spirit led him to practise around the world with stops in coastal and northern British Columbia, New Zealand, Sweden, South Africa, Uganda and Honduras. Later in his medical career he followed me into anaesthetic practice, training in Vancouver and at the Hospital for Sick Children in Toronto. Ken's Scottish determination propelled him to Department Head of Anaesthesia at the University of British Columbia Hospital.

While practising in Smithers, B.C. in 1953, Ken met and married Nancy Owens, a nurse and, like Ken, someone who loved skiing, mountaineering, hiking and travel. They had two sons, both physicians, and a daughter who now nurses at the hospital in Smithers.

Ken's early sojourn in general practice in Scotland sparked a lifelong love of the Gaelic language as profound as his love of the *pibroch mhor*, the Great Highland bagpipe. When I married, he piped my wife and me away on our honeymoon ... but not before tying a herring to my car's exhaust manifold. Thirty years later he piped at the wedding of our third son.

His outdoor adventures around the world provided an endless fund of stories, though they usually had to be coaxed out of him and were told in his typical, self-deprecating way. Climbing Mount Kilimanjaro with one of his sons, finding himself as the only guard for 5000 German POWs in the Middle East during the Second World War, and rescuing a mountain climbing companion who had suffered a heart attack were among my favourites.

Ken always prided himself on his physical fitness and often put that fitness to the test, competing in the Vancouver International, London, U.S. Marine Corps and Boston marathons while in his sixties. So it came as a great shock to his many friends and colleagues when, on June 19, 1998, Ken died after a brief illness.

Along with the Gaelic and the pipes, Ken inherited a love of boats from the country of his youth. Accordingly, in the early 1990s, he commissioned construction of a 14-foot, cedar rowing boat, which he christened the *Morag Anne*. At the age of 66 he set out alone to row from Jericho Beach in Vancouver 500 miles north through the Inside Passage to Prince Rupert.

It was a remarkable feat by a remarkable man whom I was proud to call friend.

Dr. Hugh Macartney
Victoria, B.C.
February, 1999

* * *

I have been blessed with forty years of fabulous friendship with Ken Leighton.

We met in North Vancouver where, as I worked to establish my specialist practice, I first tasted his Scottish humour and love of the Gaelic language. Ken would often send me witty requests for consults, one of which was written entirely in Gaelic. I evened the score by sending him my findings written, with the help of a friend, in Japanese.

Over the ensuing years our families grew close. We visited often, explored mountains and lakes together, shared dimly lit cabins through cold, winter nights and cared for one another.

Ken could be notoriously stubborn, was unflappable in the face of adversity, and loved a good argument. He was a strongly-built man with natural athletic ability. Even in his sixties he regularly entered some of the world's most strenuous marathons, so his decision to row from Vancouver to Prince Rupert was entirely within character.

I never dreamt he would predecease me. I will miss him sorely.

Dr. Ken Cambon
Vancouver, B.C.
April, 1999

Acknowledgements

From the launch of the boat to the launch of the book has taken almost 10 years. Along the way so many have helped. Our heartfelt thanks are extended to Greg and Shea Foster, Dan Flynn, Mr. and Mrs. Mike Sacht, Fred Sacht, Robert Charleson (*Mandala*), Jack Darlen, Jerry Arnet (*Blue Sea*), Walter and Maxine Goad (*Eight by Ten*), Ian and Vivienne Falconer (*Lycon*), Jeff Foott (*Rosebud*), Mik and Barb Endrody (*Wanderbird*), John and Noel Myers (*Nonpareil*), the crews of *Dulcinea* and *Puffin*, Dr. Ian Kennedy of Campbell River, Derick (the diver), Pat Davidson of the Minstrel Island Post Office, Len McPhee of Bones Bay, Mary Ann Snowden, Fred Apstein (Silva Bay Shipyard School), David W. Stookey (*Open-Water Rowing*), Ian Mackenzie, shipwright, Matt Murphy (*WoodenBoat*), Dr. Hugh Macartney, Dr. Ken Cambon and R.O. Malin (The Sobay Company).

The Leighton family

Oar & Sail

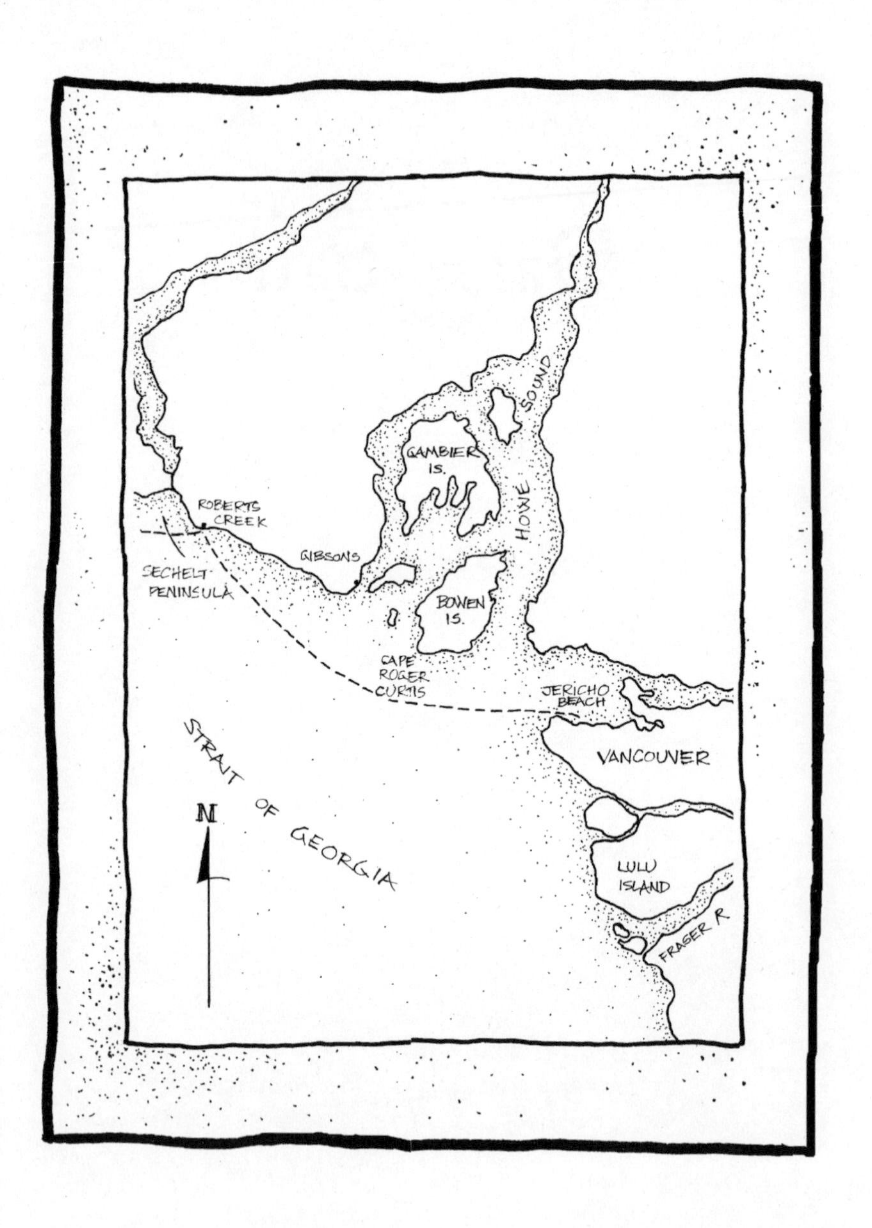
GAMBIER IS.
HOWE SOUND
ROBERTS CREEK
GIBSONS
SECHELT PENINSULA
BOWEN IS.
CAPE ROGER CURTIS
JERICHO BEACH
VANCOUVER
STRAIT OF GEORGIA
N
LULU ISLAND
FRASER R

Chapter One

It is an ancient Mariner
And he stoppeth one of three.
'By thy long gray beard and glittering eye,
Now wherefore stopp'st thou me?'
S. T. Coleridge,
THE RIME OF THE ANCIENT MARINER

IT IS EARLY morning on a grey, misty day at the end of June, 1991. The clouds may burn away or they may stay all day. This is Vancouver, no one can be sure what the day will bring. At six a.m. the weatherman was hedging his bets.

I sit in a small wooden boat, off the pier at Jericho Beach in English Bay. I am waiting for Nancy. She will bring whatever I forgot to stow on *Morag Anne* when we launched last night. It was all done in such a rush; helping hands had to be mobilised and taken with the boat on its trailer to False Creek in time to catch the top of the flood tide. It will be remarkable if everything is aboard my little boat.

An early cyclist appears on the wharf.

"That's a pretty little boat. Build it yourself?"

"Alas no, Greg Foster on Galiano Island, he built her." I row closer to the wharf to let him see the fine workmanship. "I'm glad you like her. This is her maiden voyage."

"Is that right? How far?"

This is agony. Must I tell him?

"I hope to get to Prince Rupert."

"Rupert, eh. Boy, that's a long way but I guess your boat looks like she can handle it. I sure envy you. Good luck." He rides off into the morning mist.

I know the boat can make it. The question is, can I?

Morag Anne is fourteen feet long and her beam is over five feet. She gets her name from the second daughter we never had. I used to be a dab hand at finding names for children, my own and other people's, so I had one in readiness for a daughter who failed to put in an appearance as matters turned out.

My boat is a replica, scaled down from twenty-three feet, of the launch, ship's boat or jollyboat, any of the names will do, sailed by Captain William Bligh from Tofua to Timor, after the famous mutiny in 1789. Because of the mutiny and a number of fanciful misrepresentations, Bligh has a poor name. Popular opinion is that he was an impossible disciplinarian whose harsh treatment of the crew of the *Bounty* made the mutiny almost inevitable. Putting popular opinion aside, everyone who knows anything about sailing and the sea has to admit that he must have been a superb navigator and a commander of superior ability. He sailed thousands of miles, charting the coast of Australia as he went, in an open boat with eighteen men, surviving typhoons, hunger and thirst. He lost but one man who was stoned to death at the first beach they reconnoitered, right at the start of the epic voyage.

In truth, Bligh was no more harsh a commander than other seventeenth century naval officers. It was his great misfortune to have Fletcher Christian on the lower deck, that strange, paranoid and enigmatic figure who set the mutiny in motion after the *Bounty* left the *dolce far niente* and lax discipline of the beaches of Tahiti.

My boat is made of red and yellow cedar. There is a small foredeck and an absolutely minuscule deck behind the sternsheets. Both give some shelter for my gear but absolutely none for me, of course. There is a single, unstayed mast for a standing lug sail and a tiny jib. If you don't know the lug sail, it is an almost square sail such as the conventional old sailing ships carried in the days of Nelson. It hangs from a pole called the yard and is, as we say, loose-footed. In other words, there is no boom such as you see on a modern, fore- and aft-rigged yacht. Nothing to strike the head of the unwary helmsman. The lug sail is nearly as old as time and is about the safest rig you can think of.

Morag Anne sails well before the wind but rather poorly otherwise which is what you would expect from a boat with neither centreboard nor keel.

For those readers who know the lug sail, this is boring information. I must point out, however, that sailing is pretty much a luxury and a bonus on *Morag Anne*. It's great to get the sail up but it isn't often that the wind, if there is any, is coming from the right direction. That's just a fact of life on this coast. I can't say it bothers me much. I like to row.

When the boat is fully loaded for cruising, I am moving about six or seven hundred pounds. This is the reason that I make no more than two nautical miles an hour in calm conditions. With a following tide or wind I do better than this; when either or both are against me, much less. If the wind is strong from ahead or if the tidal stream against me is more than two knots there is nothing for it but to anchor and wait for things to change. This sort of thing is what makes patience both a virtue and a necessity in small boat cruising. It is, as they say, good for the soul.

I have absolute trust in my boat's seaworthiness. Greg Foster built her with loving care, as he does all his work. I can't count the times I have been asked if I built her myself. Each time my reply is the same. I couldn't possibly build anything that would come close to his standard. He is a master shipwright and a philosopher in wood.

Greg is a most interesting man. Like me, he is not very tall, not small but not tall. He has a bowl of greying hair, the liveliest eyes and the almost lost art of listening. He listens a lot and says little. To spend some time with him is benison for the soul. He was clearly put on this earth to work with wood and to build boats. He knows what he wants to do and how he wants to live. That's not so unusual you may say, but what sets him apart is that he lives as he wants and does the work he loves. Not many of us can say that.

Forty years ago I left the Outer Hebrides in Scotland. My first home in Canada was Alert Bay which, as you may know, is the only settlement on tiny Cormorant Island in Queen Charlotte Sound, close to the northern coast of Vancouver Island. The voyage from Vancouver introduced me to our wonderful coast. I said then that one day I would

"HE WAS CLEARLY PUT ON THIS EARTH
TO WORK WITH WOOD AND TO BUILD BOATS."

have my own boat and explore it properly. This is the story of a dream that came true.

* * *

Now in English Bay, Nancy is at the pier. The only thing I forgot to load last night was a packet of plastic bags. She tosses them into the boat. There is not much to be said. I am pleased she is there to see me start. I think it is a relief to us both that the adventure is under way at last. The oars are in the water, Nancy waves. I give a nod and a grin and pull hard.

Burrard Inlet is a calm black millpond and one by one the well-known markers slip past. An eagle sits on a barnacled canister buoy watching *Morag Anne* glide by at an oar's length. His eyes are steady, his gaze unblinking and there is something feathery and still in his talons. From a freighter at anchor in the bay comes a long mournful note. Circumstances conspire to create depression and melancholy but fail in the face of my unquenchable and maybe even irrational optimism.

Rowing is warm work. I am wearing too much. Off with watch cap, parka and sweater. The last harbour marker is the bell-buoy; we reach it in what seems to me to be remarkably good time.

As ever, there is the great internal debate, to glove or not to glove. As ever, it is probably a waste of time, for blisters are almost a foregone conclusion. However, always hopeful, I have decided to experiment with fingerless cycling mittens which have well-padded palms. Alas, by the bell-buoy it is clear they are no answer. Already blisters are forming on the fingers. Worse yet, a horrid black dye is leaching from the mittens. Off with the things. Let nature or fate or whatever take her course.

But no matter. Rowing is easy, the leather collars of the oars are slick with Vaseline. I rock comfortably on the cushioned thwart with every stroke, and *Morag Anne* slips along easily, slapping gently at small waves as we meet the Fraser River's stream coming around Point Grey.

It's a long way to Alert Bay and twice as far to Prince Rupert, but time and distance are not worth thinking about. The sun is coming out. I have no deadlines. It's great to be alive.

A word about the oars. They are nine feet long, heavy-loomed, tapered and straight-bladed. As to the weight, this is nothing of course, for they are balanced exactly in the oarlocks so that their weight is unimportant. Straight blades are conventional and are certainly what Vancouver, Cook and Bligh would recognize if they could join me today.

Some people have suggested that I should take advantage of the added pulling power of spoon-bladed oars. Truth to tell, I have no experience with them. I feel intuitively that while they may be great for a racing shell in calm water they won't add anything to *Morag Anne*'s performance as we go up the coast in every sort of weather. I suppose you could say that I am as conventional as my oars. I have little or no desire to try anything different from what I know and trust.

Bowen Island is abeam. Howe Sound opens behind. This coast is a legacy of the Royal Navy, its ships and commanders, battles in far off waters, loyal recognition of kings, queens, princes and princesses as well as friends and relations and even foreign allies and enemies: the two being at times interchangeable. Captain George Vancouver and the Spanish commanders, Galiano and Valdes, sailed this coast and around Vancouver Island busily naming headlands and capes, islands and inlets, straits and passages. That they may have been named already, long before the explorers appeared on the scene, was not as important as it ought to have been.

Cape Roger Curtis slips astern and I have a strange encounter. Out of the blue comes a huge motor cruiser at high speed with a bow wave like a destroyer. It circles *Morag Anne* and stops, exhaust bubbling and gurgling, the smell of diesel filling the air. A white nautical cap calls from the flying bridge.

"Are you all right?"

I rest my oars, rocking in his swell.

"Yes, thank you."

"You're not going to have a heart attack or anything, are you?"

What a peculiar question.

"I'll try not to."

He puts his idling motor into gear and roars off at full throttle.

The sun is now beating from a cloudless sky. The sea is a copper, incandescent reflector. Back, thighs and arms feel the pleasant strain of hard work. We reach the Sechelt Peninsula, the Sunshine Coast, where weathered clapboard summer cottages fight for shoreline space with imposing mansions surrounded by impeccable lawns on which sit garden chairs from which elderly Panama-hatted gentlemen rise slowly from time to time to adjust the sprinklers that maintain the green. It is tea time.

No doubt about it, this is the Sunshine Coast indeed. When I reach Roberts Creek at last I am sunburned, parched, hungry and, above all, tired and not a little weary. This, after all, is the first day. I am knackered.

This is a good word. So good that I am driven to look for its provenance and my search takes me to the *Dictionary of Slang and Unconventional English* by Eric Partridge. Alas, Partridge tells me that I am only partly

correct to employ it here for, he says, it implies low spirits as well as fatigue. If he is right, and he must be, this is not the word for me. Exhausted I may be but my spirits are high. In fact, once the billy is boiled and the tea is made, I am on top of the world.

Partridge has pride of place in my shelf of personal deities. After surviving the horrors of the Gallipoli landings with the ANZAC brigade, he spent most of the rest of a long life in the reading room of the British Museum researching his monumental work and several treatises on the same topic. In fact, so familiar a figure was he in his shabby raincoat that the curators awarded him the unique honour and singular accolade of a permanently reserved personal desk. Short of the Order of Merit what more can a scholar aspire to?

Who dares argue with such an authority? Tired, worn, beat, exhausted but not knackered. No, not I.

The anchor is down. We are sheltered by a handy breakwater from the west wind should it come in the night. Children play on the nearby beach. Smoke curls gently from driftwood fires where parents prepare picnic suppers and I remember it is still Sunday. The future beckons.

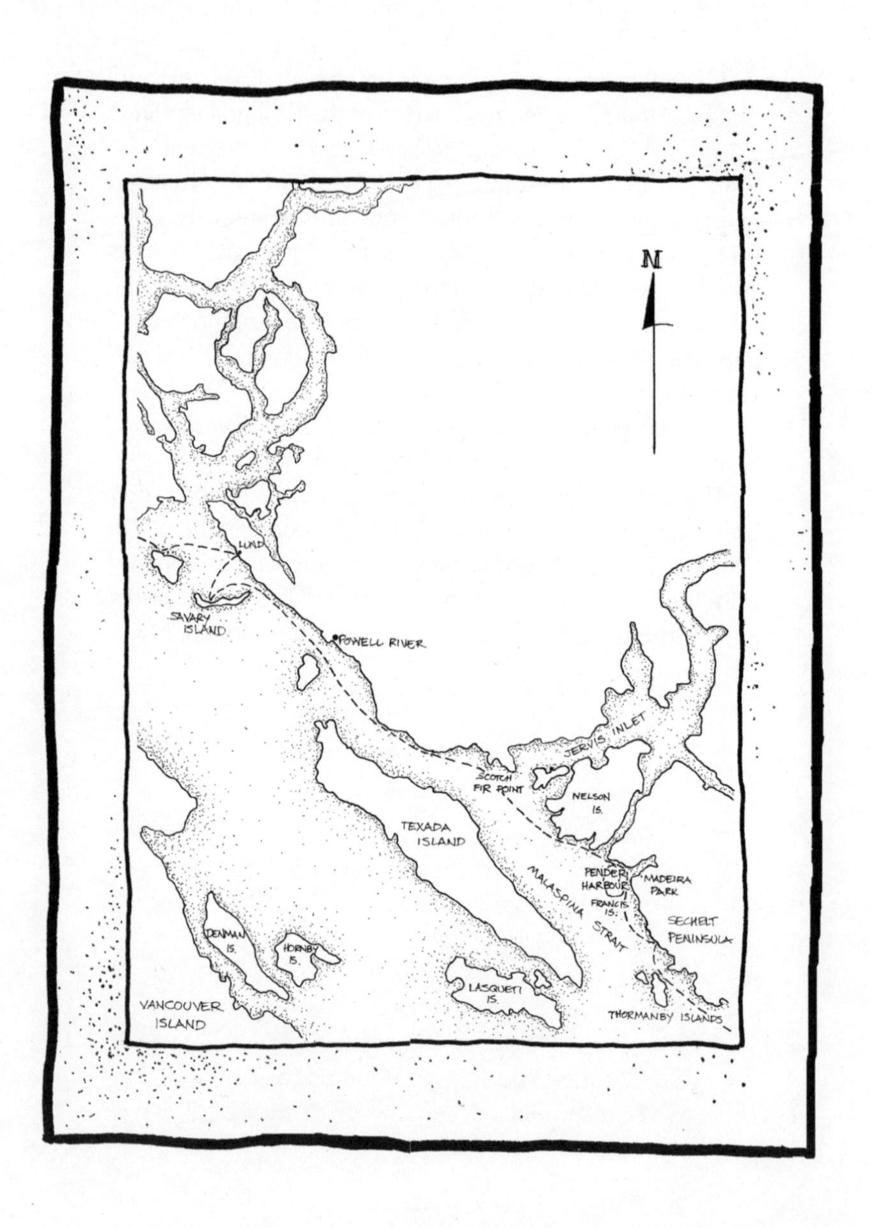
N
LUND
SAVARY ISLAND
POWELL RIVER
JERVIS INLET
SCOTCH FIR POINT
NELSON IS.
TEXADA ISLAND
MALASPINA STRAIT
PENDER HARBOUR
MADEIRA PARK
FRANCIS IS.
SECHELT PENINSULA
DENMAN IS.
HORNBY IS.
LASQUETI IS.
VANCOUVER ISLAND
THORMANBY ISLANDS

Chapter Two

There is nothing — absolutely nothing — half so much worth doing as simply messing in boats ... or with boats ... in or out of 'em it doesn't matter.
Kenneth Grahame,
THE WIND IN THE WILLOWS

TO VOYAGE IN a small boat is to travel in a self-contained world. It is altogether different from camping. In a tent you are but loosely contained, the flimsy fabric of your bivouac is no more than a cover and the environment can intrude at will. On *Morag Anne* I sleep under canvas like any camper but my little world is inviolate.

Some description is necessary concerning what may be called the domestic arrangements. During the day the tent lies under the thwart. In preparation for the night it is draped over the mainsail yard which is attached to the mast and points aft, four feet or so above the deck, the free end supported by a line from the masthead. The front of the tent is wrapped around the mast, the after end is open. Spreaders, positioned fore and aft and fastened to the gunwales, hold it taut and away from the sides of the boat. The thwart is removed and I have a living space of five by nine feet. Who could ask for more?

This may seem complicated but a more simple arrangement would be hard to discover. This is not to say that putting up the tent in the rain after a hard day of rowing, in a choppy sea, with wet decks and numb fingers is a piece of cake or a lot of fun. But if something like this bothers you a great deal all I can say is small, open boat cruising may not be for you.

I cook on a small camp stove but, truth to tell, I don't do much more than boil water for my diet is simple and I am no cook. I am well satisfied with Japanese noodles, Cream of Wheat with added raisins and homemade granola. I drink a lot of tea and coffee which taste better at sea, in the open air, than anywhere else in the world.

The head or toilet is, of course, a bucket.

Two days after leaving Roberts Creek I am tied to a wharf at Irving's Landing in Pender Harbour. The night before, I passed up the chance of a comfortable night at Smuggler Cove and pushed on against a freshening wind and contrary tide, arguing that four o'clock was too early to quit for the day. In a couple of hours I found myself completely exhausted and lucky to find a tiny cove. A noisy arc welding shop was on one side, a busy, dusty highway close by. Even mosquitoes in millions did not stop me dropping anchor. I was whacked, very close to being knackered in fact.

Now, it happened that the great Hugh Macartney of Victoria, whom God preserve, had presented me with a curiously shaped parcel, wrapped in plastic, bound with duct tape and marline. He gave it to me just before I set off. "This is for dire emergencies only," he said. As I lay on the deck, completely done in with the effort of putting the tent up, I said to myself, "This is an emergency if ever there was one," and set about opening the parcel, taking great care despite my fatigue to preserve the marline which, as any sailor knows, is hard to come by these days and is worth its weight in gold.

I found roughly the following, for I ate as I opened, making no inventory: a slab of Royal Navy chocolate (instant energy), tinned fruit, sardines, U.S. Army K Ration, cheese, biscuits and, joy upon joy, a bottle of malt whisky, Glenlivet no less, which has been known to raise the dead on more than one occasion, or so I have been told. All this bounty was wrapped inside several old copies of *Blackwood's Magazine.*

It's sad that *Blackwood's* became a victim of the times for it was a venerable Edinburgh publication. Many of us, former subscribers, treasure back numbers if only to remind ourselves how well the amateur can write when he or she has an interesting tale to tell. Many of the articles and stories were contributed from what used to be known as the Outposts of the Empire. In fact, as the Empire declined so did *Blackwood's.*

This night, however, I put *Blackwood's* on one side and apply myself to the victuals and, not least, to the Water of Life, Glenlivet. This proved a benign restorative. Despite arc welding, highway traffic and mosquitoes, I enjoyed eight hours of oblivion.

A squally following wind and rain showers blew me up channel towards Pender Harbour next morning. The following seas made *Morag Anne* yaw and slew erratically. I was forced into a basin behind Francis Island where I anchored. Since I had to wait for the flood tide to get ahead, under a small bridge and through a narrow and now dry channel, I decided to go ashore in the tiny inflatable plastic dinghy sitting in a bag under the foredeck. I felt mildly ridiculous, hunched over my knees and flailing with miniature oars towards the pebbled shore. I don't think anyone was watching which was just as well.

Silent in rubber boots, I came up behind a pair of very English-looking ladies in tweeds which were eminently suitable for this drizzly day. I had not been deceived by appearances. English they most certainly proved to be, English and charming, of a certain age, conversing in clear, modulated tones. I announced my presence with a cough.

"Is this," I asked, "Pender Harbour?"

"Not exactly. It's Madeira."

"... AND, JOY UPON JOY, A BOTTLE OF MALT WHISKY, GLENLIVET NO LESS, WHICH HAS BEEN KNOWN TO RAISE THE DEAD ON MORE THAN ONE OCCASION..."

Madeira? Well, that is a turn up. The last time I thought about Madeira it wasn't anywhere near Pender Harbour.

"Madeira Park, actually," said the smaller of the two.

"Yes, Madeira Park," said the other.

After about a half mile walk through deep cedars I passed a large school and came to a store where there was also a public phone. I called Nancy and reassured her that I was still alive and well. Inside the store I wandered around the shelves trying to think what I could possibly need and found nothing. I must admit I don't like these places, with their mindless muzak and vacant-faced citizens pushing wire carts around and almost absent-mindedly plucking items from the groaning shelves. I admit I am prejudiced but I long for the old-fashioned grocery store where you asked the proprietor for what you wanted and heeded his advice about what was good. So be it.

Suddenly I was seized with that anxiety that grips a young mother when she is separated from her child. What if the wind got up and *Morag Anne* drifted on shore, or worse yet, out of the harbour?

I took to my heels and ran. It was unfortunate, perhaps, that my route was past the school where the children were in the process of being released for the day. As they lined the fence and I ran past, parka flying and sea boots flapping, they shouted encouragement. At least, I think it was encouragement.

Of course, *Morag Anne* was exactly as I had left her.

Tied to a wharf at Irving's Landing in Pender Harbour I spend a night of incessant rain, the spreader end banging gently on the decking with every wavelet. There are plenty of these as many boats come in for fuel in the course of the night.

Campers know how pleasant it can be to sit in a tent, snug and dry, listening to the rain on the canvas. It is twice as much fun on a small boat. Duffel bag as pillow, I am reclining against the mast listening to the merry sound of the billy boiling when two curious faces peer through the tent's open end.

"Goodness me, there really is someone in there," says the lady.

"Hi there," says the man.

"Just me," say I.

The next day starts off wet and warm with clouds almost at water level. Rowing in oilskins is hot work. It isn't long before I am as wet with sweat as I would have been had I started to row in the rain wearing my usual shorts and shirt, but, stubborn to the last, I keep the things on. Happily, a brisk breeze comes to blow me up the channel, past Jervis Inlet and Scotch Fir Point, with gloomy, dark Texada Island on my port side. I can throw off the oilskins. The sails are up, a following sea hisses beside the gunwale. This is living.

It is just as well that we make such good and enjoyable time as far as Powell River for once I get there the sun comes out with a vengeance and the wind drops completely away. From there to Savary Island it is a long, tedious row but worth the effort, every creak of muscle and every drop of sweat. Savary is beautiful, a perfect gem. I anchor near the shore, inside the curve of a sandy bay looking up the strait. I hope I am not too close to the beach; the houses are close to high water mark and I don't imagine the owners are keen on wayfarers anchoring in front of their picture windows. On the other hand they won't often see a boat like *Morag Anne* nor a rig like my incomparable boat tent.

I seem to end each day's account with a comment about how hard it has been and how tired I am. Some days are harder than others and in just the same way some evenings are perfect, absolute bliss and this is one of them. The sun sets behind the distant Vancouver Island mountains, the sea is like a sheet of polished brass. I am filled with Japanese noodles, tea and biscuits; my blisters give me no pain. Were I a smoking man I dare say I would light a cigar out of sheer content with life.

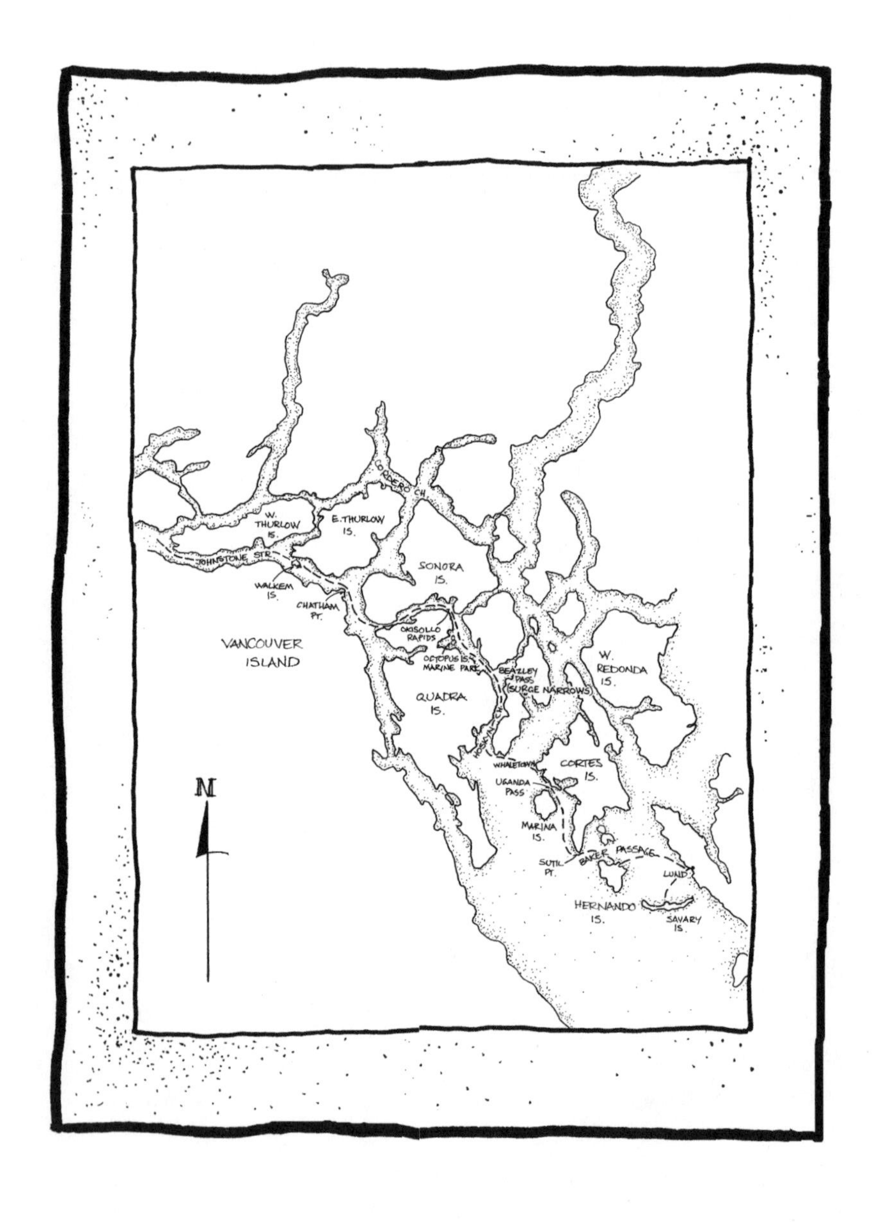
CORDERO CH.
W. THURLOW IS.
E. THURLOW IS.
JOHNSTONE STR.
SONORA IS.
WALKEM IS.
CHATHAM PT.
VANCOUVER ISLAND
OKISOLLO RAPIDS
OCTOPUS IS. MARINE PARK
BEAZLEY PASS (SURGE NARROWS)
W. REDONDA IS.
QUADRA IS.
HOSKYN CH.
WHALETOWN
CORTES IS.
UGANDA PASS
MARINA IS.
SUTIL PT.
BAKER PASSAGE
LUND
HERNANDO IS.
SAVARY IS.
N

Chapter Three

To travel hopefully is a better thing than to arrive, and the true success is to labour.
Robert Louis Stevenson,
EL DORADO

NOT TO BE outdone by Vancouver and his officers, the Canadian Hydrographic Service has done excellent work mapping this coast. Their maps aren't cheap but worth every cent. On bigger boats than mine they are spread on chart tables, open to their fullest extent. I must be content with folding and refolding them until only the part of immediate interest is in front of me. I then put it in a transparent, waterproof container. A magnifying glass is useful for looking at details which may not be important to the average sailor in a large boat.

Quite as important as a chart is the book of tides and currents. In fact, it is an absolute necessity. Bigger boats than *Morag Anne* have to pay attention to tides, of course, but I have to use them and their associated currents. If I don't, I shan't make much headway. A surgeon who tried to train me once said, "Anyone can be a hindrance, try to be a help." Finding good help anywhere is a combination of skill, art and luck.

I decide to call in at Lund when I leave Savary next morning. The coast is fog-bound and notwithstanding my excellent chart, I have no option but to head in its general direction and look for the entrance to the harbour. I make for the other side of the strait but forget to check my tide tables and am carried to the south by a fast running stream. Indeed I am a considerable distance off course before I realize what has happened. As a result I have a hard row against the current before I can slip into the harbour. Very exasperating and very unnecessary. A couple of fishermen have anchored their little run-about not far from the entrance and watch my struggle in some wonder. Where, they must have asked themselves, is his outboard?

So far, I have come from Burrard Inlet, into the Gulf of Georgia, through Welcome Passage and into Malaspina Strait. In Welcome Passage I passed Merry Island and the two Thormanby Islands, all of them momentos of the 1860 Derby, not the Kentucky Derby but the original one at Epsom in England. As usual, they were named by an officer in the Royal Navy but, for a change, not to honour an admiral, a battle or a member of the royal family. The 1860 Derby was won by a horse named Thormanby owned by a Mr. Merry, and when the news reached *HMS Plumper*, where he was on survey duty, I suppose it was very welcome. Possibly the captain had a wager riding on the result. The gulf was named by Vancouver in honour of his king, who was George the Third, and Malaspina was an Italian captain in the service of Spain and famous enough for Galiano and Valdes to name an inlet in his honour and for Captain Richards of the *Plumper* to attach it to the strait seventy years later. Lund was so named by the two Thulin brothers who settled there, in honour of their home town in faraway Sweden.

The wharf at Lund is crammed with fishing boats. On the oil-stained water floats orange peel, eggshell and other debris that is both sinister and unsanitary in appearance. Insinuating *Morag Anne* between two gill-netters I begin to wonder why I have bothered to come to Lund in the first place. And then I meet a very pleasant Indian girl with a diminutive cherub at her skirt. She is full of smiles although the cherub clings tightly and looks at me with suspicion. Lund Harbour doesn't seem such a hole in the wall after all.

"Are you looking for fresh water?" she asks.

Aha, I think, that's why I came here. I was sure there must have been a reason. I haven't used all of my original five gallons but it is getting stale and I have to admit that small animalcula are floating around inside the container. I thank my good Samaritan, she takes my bow line, fastens it adroitly to the wharf and directs me to a tap that is hiding behind a heap of nets halfway down the wharf.

I buy some bandaids in the general store. They are no longer needed. Good, hard callus covers the current crop of blisters but on the good old principle "you never know" they seem a good buy. In any case I am the store's only customer and after wandering completely through it, looking at every shelf, I feel I ought to buy something, even a token something. Whether or not the young person at the cash register is pleased is impossible to tell, but she does shift her bubblegum from one cheek to the other as she takes my money.

Out on Malaspina Strait once again, making for Hernando Island, it is blisteringly hot. The sea is an oily calm with a little swell. I put these conditions next to a sideways chop in my list of rowing dislikes. It's not that I get seasick, perish the thought. I suppose it is mostly a matter of downright boredom and ennui.

Hernando Cortes, the conquistador, was brave, brutal and lucky. He was also perfidious. He pretended to befriend the emperor, Montezuma, and then betrayed his trust. He deserted his Indian lover and accomplice in this act of treachery. But his was a brutal age. Cortes was alone in a vast land with no more than a handful of men and a few horses. It was a situation of extreme peril and we have to give a devil his due: the conquest of Mexico was an achievement nonpareil. So, I'll let him have the beautiful little island that bears his name. Why not?

The islet is a jewel in the sun when I drop my anchor in the bay among a fleet of run-abouts gently bobbing at their moorings. Children play on a soft, sandy beach, watched by mothers and possibly nannies from deck chairs and blankets. The arrival of a small wooden boat causes no stir, makes no impression, is probably not noticed at all.

Like Savary Island, Hernando is a well kept secret and is even more remote from the urban Lower Mainland of the province. Lucky cottagers and holiday-homeowners, I envy you but not too much, not enough to exchange my nomadic *Morag Anne* for all your unspoiled beauty and peace.

The beach looks eastward, and when the sun sinks behind the high clay cliffs and forest shadows claim the strand, mothers, nannies and children pick up their belongings, or such as they can find, and slowly make their way to cottages, holiday homes and some imposing mansions. They leave the beach to the eagles and to me.

There is a faint westerly breeze as I raise the tent. By the time I have eaten my noodles it is more than a breeze. An unpleasant chop comes at *Morag Anne* from several directions at once. She bobs, shakes and tosses. It is going to be a disturbed night and it is, as usual, all my own fault for I have ignored the pilot book's warning that the anchorage is relatively unprotected. Fools rush in where angels fear etc. etc. Shortly after midnight I take down the tent but this does not help and as soon as there is enough light to see where I am going, I raise anchor and am off.

It is a fine morning. As I cross Baker Passage, towards Sutil Point on Cortes Island, a tug towing two scows filled with sawdust hoots at me. Of course there is no chance that I would cross his path, but I don't blame him for not knowing that *Morag Anne* has no auxiliary power. I give a wave, on the assumption that someone will see me.

The *Sutil* and the *Mexicana* were Galiano's ships. The Spanish and British were charting the coast at roughly the same time. Galiano sailed in the *Sutil* and Valdes commanded the sister schooner *Mexicana.* Vancouver's ship, the *Discovery*, was accompanied by the armed brig *Chatham* which was first captained by Broughton. Zachary Mudge, 1st lieutenant of the *Discovery*, was sent back to England September 30, 1792 from Nootka, by way of China. Broughton was sent from Monterey on a similar mission in January of 1793. These are all well-known names for any West Coaster.

Uganda Pass, between Marina and Cortes (I am going to stop writing 'island' every time) is so narrow at low water that I wonder if I will get through it until I meet a sloop, *Shikari*, which has just come through, ghosting along in the lightest of airs, conned most adroitly by a helmsman who obviously knows his business. I can see someone taking a photograph of *Morag Anne* and I sit up straight and try to look nonchalant.

I scrape through with a couple of feet to spare on either side. The sun is murderous. I make for Whaletown on Cortes.

Whaletown, terminal for the ferry to Heriot Bay on Quadra, does not look the most tempting anchorage when first I see it but it is there or nowhere. The worst sort of sea for rowing has developed, with waves coming at the boat broadside, short, steep waves in quick succession. We roll and rock, sometimes the blades of the oars are deep in the water and sometimes they pull nothing but air.

I row around the harbour looking for a good place to drop the anchor. Nowhere seems completely satisfactory and finally I give up and anchor near, too near, the ferry landing and turn in early, expecting the worst. I am surprised to waken in the early morning after a superb, quiet night and to find the ferry, *Nimpkish*, berthed within spitting distance. I haven't heard a sound. God is good.

It is only five o'clock but the sun is warm, the bay like glass and not another creature moves apart from dragonflies swooping over driftwood and sea-wrack on the shore. I gently pull up anchor and slip silently from the bay.

I am making for Surge Narrows, the waterway, not the settlement of the same name.

To understand what happens next you have to appreciate one very simple fact that has to do with the Pacific Ocean, tides and Vancouver Island. Everyone knows that tides rise and fall, or in nautical terms flood and ebb. If you think of the Pacific as a big saucer you realise that when the water level rises on the west coast of North America it is because it is falling on the other side of the ocean. Vancouver Island is a huge barrier to this gradient, the tide rising on its west side first. It then surges around both the north and south ends of the island. This means that there must be a point on its east coast where two tidal streams meet, one flooding in from the north above, and one from the south below. This is as elementary as it seems.

Over the broad expanse of the Pacific the tidal stream is negligible but in narrow waters it is another story. Surge Narrows is a good example. Sailing on the West Coast necessitates a knowledge of tidal currents. Times and strength are found in a book of tables and direction is shown on charts by arrows. Direction of flooding is indicated by feathers on the arrow shaft.

When I set off towards Surge Narrows, up Hoskyn Channel, I check the direction of flood tide. The feathered arrows point north.

Beazley Pass, Surge Narrows is a gloomy looking place. At least, it is gloomy the day I am there. The clouds are low, a light rain is falling, the sea is black. Although it is a flat calm there are mysterious looking swirls all about. Barnacled rocks line the passage and, in a tiny bay at the entrance, kelp moves listlessly to and fro'.

I don't know what it is, but somehow I have a feeling that there is something menacing about the place. Once more I check the tables and the chart. No problem. It is the end of slack water. In about half an hour the flood will start. Oh, well. Nothing for it but to launch forward into the pass and off I set.

Everything is fine for a few moments, a very few moments. Then, with surprising suddenness, the flood tide begins. It comes with a whoosh and a roar and — what is this? It is coming from the wrong direction. We are swept into the little bay, caught in a whirlpool and spinning out towards the main channel which by this time is a maelstrom. I lean over the side and manage, by sheer luck, to grasp a bit of kelp and, by a chance that is just as lucky, the kelp doesn't pull loose. We spin round and round, my death grip on the slimy, slippery but ever so God-sent kelp, the only thing between me and perdition.

Then, inevitably, the fragile strand parts. At once we are spun around and swept at the same time out towards the main stream where logs, roots and whole trees toss and bounce around in a jumble. The current can reach twelve knots in Surge Narrows and I have a feeling it is near its maximum.

In desperation I leap forward and throw out the anchor. To my great relief it takes hold, and I give silent thanks to Greg Foster for insisting on a five-kilogram Bruce anchor which, on the face of it, had seemed far too much for such a small boat as *Morag Anne.*

Gripped by the whirlpool, the boat spins around and around the anchor chain. It is no comfort to notice the outer edge of the whirlpool is higher than the transom. I sit on the thwart making feeble and futile stabs with the oars

in an attempt to slow things down. It is a useless gesture but it warms me a little. The rain is coming down in icy sheets. I don't dare to get into my heavy foul weather gear lest I end up in the water and have to try and swim ashore. Now I come to think of it, I could just as well have put everything on for my chances of survival were pretty slim, naked or dressed.

I spend more than five hours in that wretched spot. Five hours of prolonged fear and terror. I can truthfully say I have never in my life been so frightened for so long.

A huge cabin cruiser comes along from the north. It sweeps past at terrific speed, rolling alarmingly in the narrows. At Hoskyn Channel it is caught in a massive whirlpool and cants over on its side, careening for what must have been an agonizing moment for all on board.

As the current slackens, impatience overcomes caution and I pull the anchor up and set off, too early it turns out. It is a struggle to win through the narrow gut of the pass and, what with one thing and another, an exhausted ancient mariner eventually anchors in the first bay he comes to, puts up his tent and sleeps like a log for ten hours.

Examining the chart next morning, I find the explanation for what at the time had seemed the weird behaviour of flood tide. When I come to plan the day's journey and look towards Okisollo Rapids, the next hazard, I discover that the flood tide comes from the north. All is made clear. Rather late, perhaps, but no more mystery. As usual, it is my own fault. I could have discovered the point of flood reversal by reading the *Coastal Pilot*. I determine not to repeat the mistake.

Flood tides would come from the north until Vancouver Island is behind me. I row to Octopus Islands Marine Park confident that I will pass through the next rapids on an ebbing tide.

But confidence is an uncertain quantity and waxes and wanes most strangely. I admire those who, as it seems, make a resolve and put action to it without qualm or concern. After my experience at Surge Narrows this is definitely not me. I am delighted to find a large cabin cruiser at anchor in the marine park. The pleasant looking man at the taffrail, enjoying the morning sun, has a solid, confident, knowledgeable air and I don't hesitate to ask his advice about the tides at Okisollo. I find myself somewhat at a disadvantage in this discussion inasmuch as I can't lay hands on my reading glasses. You might think that you couldn't lose anything so thoroughly in the confines of a very limited space in a very small boat. I must say, however, if you believe that you are very mistaken. A man should always have a magnifying glass ready at hand for such an emergency when he reaches that age where his arms aren't long enough to accommodate the changes in near vision that time's inexorable passage brings.

My new friend and I, he looking at his own tide tables and I thinking mostly and, as it transpires, too much about the Surge Narrows fiasco to pay close attention, agree that at about an hour after mid-day the rapids will be starting a period of slack water, the ideal time, in other words, for *Morag Anne* to slip through without any bother.

The sun is shining, the sea is calm and serene. In several bays yachts are anchored, crews and skippers taking their ease on a cloudless morning. Octopus Marine Park is a series of small islands, an idyllic spot for the coastal cruiser.

But hist, as the old books say, what is this noise I hear? As I draw near the rapids there is an ominous sound, like an approaching express, the same sound that I listened to for those agonizing hours yesterday. In a moment or two and when it is almost too late to pull back, I find myself on the edge of yet another maelstrom. The flood tide is coming through the rapids full speed ahead and bearing its complement of tossing timber, trees and debris. To get back to the safety of the park is the objective; this is no time to try to understand what went wrong. And getting back isn't all that simple. Luckily there is something of a back eddy just inside the kelp line, and with the help of this I claw my way. Quite exhausted as well as baffled, I am only too pleased to drop anchor in a snug cove. I put the tent up just before a downpour starts, a minor triumph that goes some way towards restoring my equanimity. Noodles bubbling over the stove, rain hissing on the water and drumming on the tent, I am as happy as Larry, whoever Larry is or was.

Partridge says the term comes from Australia, that fount of colourful slang, but that's all he has to say which is unusual for him. As a rule he makes an informed guess. On the question of Larry's pedigree he is silent.

My glasses come to light, I read the tide tables with great care and look at the chart. My cruising friend and I couldn't have been more wrong. There it is, in black and white. "Flooding at twelve thirty." No room for discussion. What got into us will ever be a mystery.

Early next day, with mist rising from the sea and surrounded by seals, I pass through the rapids without any trouble. The seals pay *Morag Anne* not the slightest bit of attention. I am intrigued to note they appear to play with their visibly expired air like children on a frosty morning.

Along the shores of Cordero Channel are many areas of clear-cut logging, recent and not so recent. These give the place a look of Passchendaele or the Somme in the First World War, the one that my generation called "The Great War". I think that if only the loggers could tidy the place up after they have finished it wouldn't be so bad. Jagged stumps standing bare and desolate among the tangle of fallen timber lying every which way just serve to emphasize the rape that has taken place. I know it's hard to balance the economic advantage of timber harvesting with the preservation of the environment, and I don't pretend to have the answer to that conundrum.

Oh dear, the byways of language. Where in the world does "conundrum" come from? Onions' *Dictionary of English Etymology* admits defeat although making the suggestion that it may perhaps be a schoolboy joke for an imaginary Latin word. A bit unsatisfactory but I shall have to leave it at that.

Morag Anne and I speed down Cordero with a following tide. The channel is lined by fish farms. At one of these I come upon a delightful cottage floating on cedar logs. There is an ample deck with flowering shrubs in tubs and barrels. There is also a dog which barks as soon as he sees me. This brings a woman to the door. She waves. The barking dog, the garden shrubs and plants, neatly curtained windows, I might be in suburbia.

To my great surprise I am across Johnstone Strait by mid-morning and enjoying a second breakfast. I drink my last tin of beer in celebration, only to regret doing so when I come to rouse myself from the nap that follows. Lunch — or second breakfast — and beer, sun and a possibly unjustified sense of accomplishment is a perfect formula for forty winks but it's hard to get going again.

Johnstone, a common Scottish name, is pronounced the same way as Johnson. The 't' is silent. Don't ask me why. And, most emphatically, it is not 'JohnSTONE' as in a rock. Who was Johnstone? He was Master of the *Chatham*, Vancouver's second ship, in whose cutter he first navigated this unknown strait.

And Chatham Point is abeam in the late afternoon with its lighthouse, red-roofed buildings and, half a mile offshore, a small boat crammed to the gunwales with people, men, women and children, most of them with fishing rods and none of them wearing life jackets. One or two of them wave. I return their greetings and hurry cravenly on, leaving behind a maritime tragedy in the making.

In the evening, still carried by a following tide, I anchor in the lee of one of the Walkem Islands in the middle of Johnstone Strait. For a small, heavily laden wooden boat I have covered a prodigious distance. Hours of daylight remain but who is in a hurry? It is a fine evening, the air is warm, the sea calm and a hospitable bay beckons. The anchor is down, the tent is up and the Cream of Wheat on the boil. Nirvana.

Mr. Justice Walkem was born in Newry, Northern Ireland, in 1834. Some might think this reason enough to have small islands named after you in Johnstone Strait. I don't know about that. I hope he was a good judge.

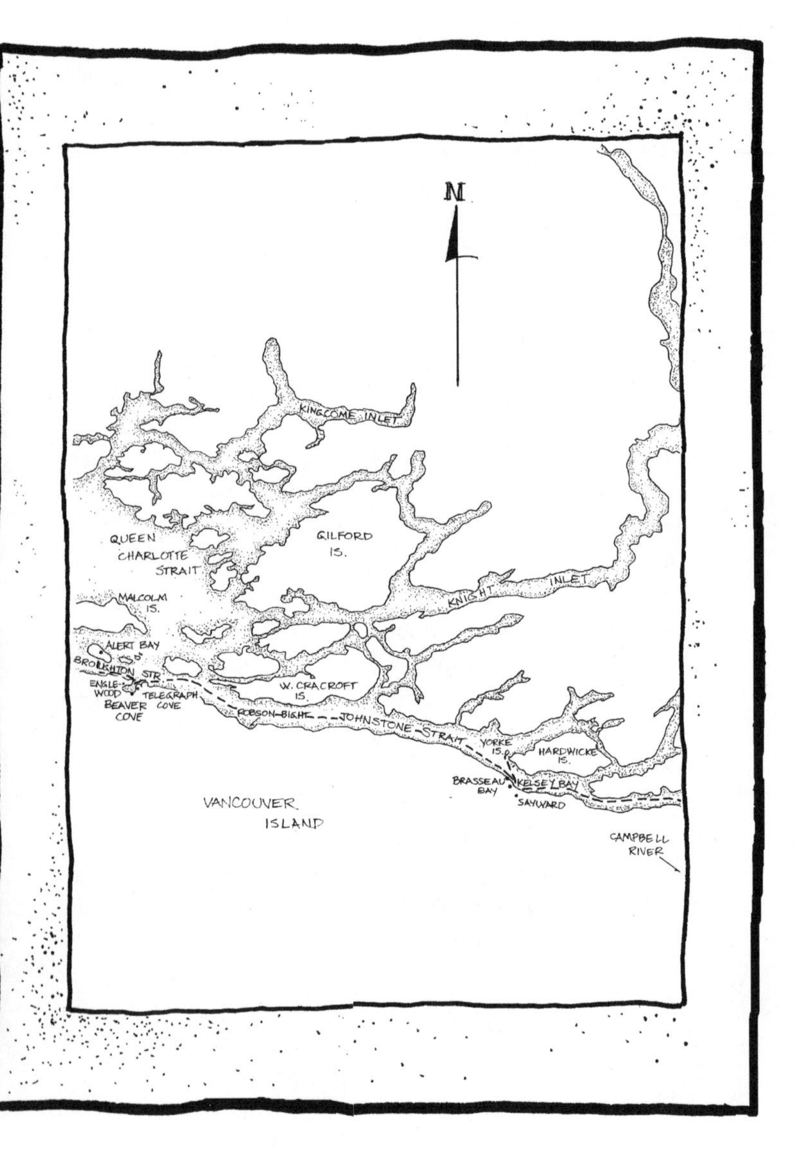
N
KINGCOME INLET
QUEEN
CHARLOTTE
STRAIT
GILFORD
IS.
KNIGHT INLET
MALCOLM
IS.
ALERT BAY
BROUGHTON STR
ENGLE-
WOOD
TELEGRAPH
COVE
BEAVER
COVE
W. CRACROFT
IS.
ROBSON BIGHT
JOHNSTONE STRAIT
YORKE
IS.
HARDWICKE
IS.
BRASSEAU
BAY
KELSEY BAY
SAYWARD
VANCOUVER
ISLAND
CAMPBELL
RIVER

Chapter Four

Obair latha ... toiseachadh.
(A day's work ... getting started.)
GAELIC SAYING

PROCRASTINATION is said to be the thief of time. Perhaps it is. But when you can let yourself go and accept your fate, it is delightful. I find it hard to tear myself away from the beautiful Walkem Islands next morning so I linger long over raising anchor and getting under way. I have no one to apologise to and not a care in the world. Not all old men can be so lucky.

Once more I am carried along by a strong tidal stream. When I come to think about it, this is highly mysterious. There can be no question about it being a flood tide for the rocks along the shore are quickly submerging. But flood tide in Johnstone Strait comes from the north and

Morag Anne is, at least in theory, beating against it. Later, I learn that I'm not the first to be puzzled by this strange phenomenon. No one has given me a satisfactory explanation, although I suppose there must be one. I'm not about to quibble. A helping hand is a helping hand and God be thanked when you get one.

The harbour of Kelsey Bay, which I reach quite early in the afternoon, is protected by a line of rusting old ships, partially submerged, scuttled, stripped and abandoned. It's not a pretty sight. I recognise the old *Cardena*, Union Steam Ship Line. I sailed in her from Vancouver to Squamish in the days before there was a highway or railroad. It is sad to see her mottled with rust, funnel gone and half submerged.

As I round the last of the hulks and make for the government wharf I see it is crowded with boats of all sorts. I nose along the lines of cruisers, yachts, launches and fishing boats looking for somewhere to tie up.

A grizzled, salt-and-pepper sort of chap, with tattooed arms and a grin, sitting on an upturned bucket on the deck of a gill-netter, calls out.

"Don't you think you're getting a bit old for that sort of thing?"

"Indeed no. You're only as old as you feel."

"A man after my own heart. Come and raft alongside of me. You won't find anything better with all these buggers. God knows where they've all come from."

And this is how I meet Mike Sacht, the self-styled bad boy of the Sacht clan of Salmon River, Sayward, Kelsey Bay and Brasseau Bay. I have good reason to bless them all, as you will learn.

I fill up my water carrier and we sit a while and chat.

"Don't think you are the first to row from Vancouver to Kelsey Bay," says Mike. "My grandfather rowed there and back twice a year fetching supplies for his store at Salmon River. And it was a big heavy boat he had, not a dainty little craft like yours."

It had not even passed through my mind that I could be the first to make such a trip and, to tell the truth, I don't care very much, so I hold my peace.

This rather aggressive defense of the honour and reputation of his grandfather completely belies the true Mike. He is the very soul of kindness and hospitality. I think I have already made plain my regard for the Sacht family in general. Mike may be the bad boy if he says so. As far as I am concerned he is a great guy and my pal and that's that.

"You're just plain lucky. You will hardly ever see the strait as calm as this. And you say you had the tide with you all day? Well, that's the way she goes around here when the weather is like this. Other times it will be just the reverse and she'll come down from the north all day and all night. There's no explaining it, that's the way she is." Then he adds, "If you're not too tired you shouldn't try to spend the night here. Row over to Yorke Island, across the strait. It's not more than a couple of miles or so. Over here it's the biggest booming grounds on the Island. Boom boats'll fart up and down all night long, hootin' an' hollerin' to beat crazy. Those buggers," gesturing to the cruisers and yachts, "won't hear a thing over the din of their own dam' generators. There's good shelter over behind Yorke, good shelter from any nor'wester and sure as shootin', that's what's comin'."

Nothing beats local advice. I am soon out on the strait heading for Yorke, which may indeed be no more than a few miles from Kelsey Bay but it is a hard pull to get there. I take the first decent looking bay I come upon and drop the anchor with relief and a certain amount of satisfaction for a well-spent day. As the billy boils for supper I note a little breeze has started to blow down the strait.

By the time the tiny dinghy is found in the mess and hodge-podge of supplies and equipment beneath the foredeck, the wind is strong enough to bend the tree tops around the bay. I set out to explore the little island. To my astonishment I immediately come upon a ring of rusting, military barbed wire. Whoever laid it did a very thorough job. I have some difficulty to get through the wretched stuff which, as I find out, goes all around the high water mark of the island. Of course, it is impossible to guess why anyone bothered to lay this barrier on Yorke Island. As far as I know, no one but the army uses this type of concertina wire that needs no fence posts for its support. I may be wrong and perhaps some very cautious, not to say malicious, owner put it down to keep trespassers away.

Waves are dashing against the north side of the island, spray and foam flecking the rocks at the top of the cliffs as I paddle back to *Morag Anne*. This goes on all night. Several times I awaken and listen to the gale as it howls through the cedars. Mike Sacht told me no lie when he said I could find good shelter for the boat does no more than rock gently at her mooring.

Morning brings a gloomy sight with grey sky, foaming breakers at the entrance and ten-foot waves hurrying down the strait. No chance at all to row a small boat in such conditions and trying to beat up the strait without a keel, centreboard or lee-boards is absolutely out of the question.

The day will not be completely wasted. Chaos can be dealt with and order restored to the mess of supplies, bedding, books, ropes, lines and impedimenta. I find several useful things that I haven't been able to lay hands on for days. When all this is done, it is pleasant to laze with *Blackwood's*, eat more than I need, pore over charts and attempt to raise the Coast Guard weather report on my tiny receiver. In this last I have no success. Yorke's forest cover blocks all reception. But the weather speaks for itself. We are in for a good blow and there is no reason why it wouldn't continue all day.

A weather forecast from Alert Bay Coast Guard may be unobtainable but it is thrilling to know I am getting close to at least one of the goals of the voyage. My spirits rise at the thought. Perhaps they get a little too much boost for, next morning, I persuade myself that the wind is less and the sea, although broken and confused, is within the bounds of possible management. I push the bow into the strait. What a mistake it is. In fact, it is also quite dangerous. Details would be tedious to recount. One rough sea must be very like another in the telling. I can't make any headway, rowing is very difficult as the boat rolls from side to side. I am lucky to get back into my cove.

I sit and stew. The sun comes out. The wind blows and I continue to stew. How long is this going to go on? Will my water hold out? How about rations? My basic menu is secure; I won't starve, but what about the bit of fruit? The more I think of supermarkets, fruit and sweet biscuits the more I regret that I hadn't stocked up at Kelsey Bay.

Any fool could see I can't proceed up Johnstone Strait in this weather. But, how about making a run back to Kelsey Bay? I make up my mind to try. The anchor is up and I am rowing into the strait before I have time for second thoughts.

Second thoughts and even third ones would have been well worthwhile, for once I am out of Yorke's shelter and with no hope or chance to get back, I am in a pickle indeed with breaking seas coming at me from every direction. Rowing is impossible for *Morag Anne* is rolling and wallowing, broaching and spinning, tiller and rudder banging helplessly to and fro' in a proper dog's breakfast of a sea.

There is nothing for it but to hoist the merest scrap of a mainsail and try to run before the gale. In a second I am racing down the strait with following seas curling under the boat and breaking all around. The danger of pitch-poling end over end or being pooped or swamped by a breaking wave is enough to take my mind off the rubber duck, the dinghy, which is still in tow. But not for long. I am forcefully reminded when the wind picks it up and hurls it aboard the boat, striking me a smart blow on the head which knocks me off the sternsheets and onto the deck. Although it does me no great harm it very nearly causes a capsize. I throw it quickly over the transom, grab the tiller and manage to get control again. It is a surprise to find that my wild ride is not quite such a mad race as before until I realize what has happened. The so-called dinghy must have been punctured in the melee; it is partly submerged and thus acts as a sea anchor. God moves in mysterious ways indeed.

Even with the drag of the sea anchor I am still moving at a great pace. Without it I would certainly sweep past the

"WHEN ALL THIS IS DONE, IT IS PLEASANT TO LAZE WITH BLACKWOOD'S..."

entrance to Kelsey Bay. As it is, I wonder if I can find the opening and be able to turn in. Suddenly, I spot an opening in the cliff just before the old hulks. The tiller is over and we shoot into calm water quicker than the thought.

What a blessed contrast. This is Brasseau Bay, calm and still, protected by high cliffs from the wind and wave. At the head of the bay is a short, rocky beach and beyond this, with a backing of tall cedars, a small white house with outbuildings. On the landward side the forest comes close to the water's edge, so close that the tips of branches brush the very surface of the bay. The seaward cliff is topped with pines and arbutus, swaying before the gale. The still air of the bay is filled with a dry, resinous scent and the sweetness of honeysuckle.

A well-built young man stands half way down the bluff. He has a child on his shoulders. Immediately beneath him runs a wharf, parallel to the shore. Prominent on its decking a large sign reads "PRIVATE. Do NOT moor here".

"Are you in trouble?"

"Not any longer. I'm glad to get in out of what's out there though."

"Well, you can tie up here if you want. Pay no attention to the sign. That's to keep away those sports fishermen who think they own the place and can moor anywhere they please. Where did you come from?"

When I tell him, omitting the saga of the dinghy, he says, "From Yorke, eh? Well, you came over the worst bit of the strait. You're lucky to have made it in that little boat."

I tie the boat to the wharf and go ashore. An elderly gentleman is coming towards me. He puts one foot down with obvious discomfort and uses a cane.

"Did you see any fish out there?"

"Not a one." I might have told him that the only fish I would have noticed would have been one that jumped aboard and wriggled in my lap. I don't.

"Be danged if I have seen any for days. Never saw a year like this. Weather's all wrong too. A nor'west wind like this, wrong time of year and likely to blow for days, I guess."

I must confess that I don't much care if it blows for ever, so happy am I to be safe and sound. I am to change my mind about that as time passes, of course.

Further conversation with this fine, sprightly old gentleman reveals that he is Mr. Fred Sacht, the patriarch of the many Sachts in and around Kelsey Bay and the uncle of the amiable Mike who greeted me as I arrived at the government wharf and advised Yorke for the night. When I recount my conversation with the self-confessed bad boy, Mr. Fred advises against putting too much store in Mike's claims.

"A great one to spin a yarn is Mike. His granddad never rowed down to Vancouver more than once a year, and he always had two or three young fellows along with him to help bring up a load of goods for the store, the first store in the Salmon River Valley. Anyway, as soon as the gas boats came in he never did no more rowing, I'll tell you."

Referring to his stick and limp, he says:

"Twisted my ankle a while back, working in the bush, me and the wife. Slipped off a knot or something. It's getting better but it's mighty slow. Went to the doctor but for all the good that did I might have stayed home. Kept me waiting an hour and did nothin'. Dam' doctors, maybe they can fix a bad heart, I don't know about that, but I sure as heck know they can't do nothin' for a little bitty sprained ankle, I tell you."

It doesn't look to me as if Mr. Fred is going to be held back for very long and, indeed, that afternoon I see him and a little lady whom I take to be his wife, working on the beach with a donkey engine. They are wrapping chokers around drift-logs and hauling them above the high water mark. He has discarded his stick and seems to get around just fine with a sort of hop and skip. Active, do-it-yourself physiotherapy I think. The best kind.

Everyone in Brasseau Bay is a Sacht or married to one. There is also a family of pet goats and another of deer, a doe and two fawns. The fawns are newborns. The doe lies panting in a cedar's shade and the fawns, not knowing any better, have no fear and graze unconcerned within a few feet of passersby.

Mr. Fred and I get well acquainted over the next day or two. A man of definite opinions, he isn't backward in letting me know that he doesn't have much time for sports fishermen, cruise ships, or the medical profession. He and his like made this coast the place it once was. I'll never measure up to them, but I enjoy being with those who still remain and they are getting fewer every year.

The northwest wind blows steadily. After four days of waiting, even the charms of Brasseau Bay begin to wilt. I would have despaired but for a good friend in Campbell River, Dr. Ian Kennedy. He drives to Kelsey Bay, takes me back to his beautiful log home, wines and dines me magnificently and drives me back after a couple of days. I know the full meaning of rest and recreation as a result of his kindness and hospitality.

In Campbell River I run into the skipper of the yacht, *Shikari*, which passed me in Uganda Pass. He confirms that he did indeed have a photograph of *Morag Anne* and promises he will send me a print. I'm pleased to say he proves as good as his word. I won't expound on the mysteries of chance or attempt to reckon the odds against such an unlikely encounter. These coincidences happen. To my mind they seem to happen to me more than to others, but I dare say I am quite mistaken there. We all like to feel we are unique.

Back in Brasseau Bay, I climb to the top of the cliff in the evening and hold my tiny weather receiver to my ear. Reception from Alert Bay Coast Guard station is very faint but, between the crackling static, I can make out the prediction that the wind is going to turn to the southeast some time the following day. That is all I need.

High tide is midnight. If I set off an hour later I will catch the ebb which should set towards the north, although I'm not counting on it inasmuch as tidal currents in Johnstone Strait have already demonstrated they have minds of their own.

It is a fine night and I don't bother to put up the tent the better to make a quick getaway. Mr. Fred bids me farewell at his front door in carpet slippers and tells me to come back any time. I sleep under the stars until it is time to leave.

What a relief to be under way again. Phosphorescent drops fall from the blades of the oars. *Morag Anne* seems to glide easily through the dark sea. God be praised, the tidal stream is in my favour at last.

A cruise ship ghosts down the strait, all lights ablaze, engines throbbing, posing no danger to a shore-hugging

small boat sailor although *Morag Anne* carries no lights. When I have to row in the dark I am extremely careful to avoid all shipping lanes and keep more than a weather eye open.

A breeze from the south comes with the morning light so I raise sail. The breeze freshens. I have a glorious time of it all morning. When the wind becomes more than a good spanking breeze and the seas are breaking in the shallow waters of Robson Bight, I pass a whale-watching boat at anchor. I cannot envy the paying customers huddled at the rail, wrapped in parkas and scarves. Some of them may have been battling sea-sickness as their boat is tossing, pitching and rolling. Sailors call this "corkscrewing" and the term is fairly apt. I give what I hope is a cheery wave as I slip past on the crest of a following sea.

I set the anchor in Beaver Cove in the early evening with more than thirty miles under my belt, a phenomenal run for any day and doubly pleasurable after the ennui and delay at Kelsey Bay. The wind is blowing half a gale when I arrive where Queen Charlotte and Johnstone Straits meet. Alert Bay is not more than two or three miles off, and if I hadn't the local knowledge and great respect for the passage, known as Broughton Strait, I believe I would have chanced the winds and the very confused rough looking sea. Call me chicken if you like. I'll counter with the memory of four local men drowning when their boom boat capsized in these same waters under our horrified gaze, forty years ago.

Beaver Cove, Telegraph Cove, Englewood, it is all familiar territory. Time is telescoped and it is as if I had been crossing yesterday by water taxi from Alert Bay to catch the train up to Nimpkish Lake or go over to visit

Fred Wasdell, my great friend, and his dad who gave me his copies of *Hansard* for my edification and interest. Those water taxi trips were, as they say, something else again. Often they were taken in the pitch darkness, in heavy rain and a quartering sea. I was inside a thin plywood hull, covered and buttoned down at countless points by a canvas cover, sitting on twin Chrysler engines and giving rather less than half an ear to the semi-coherent ramblings of the operator who had an unfortunate fondness for Lucky Lager. Unfortunate only in that he drank as he drove through the dead-head littered waters of Broughton Strait. I have always been cursed with an over vivid imagination and anticipation of the worst. The fact that I come by the last of these more than honestly is no support either.

The coast was booming then: from small hand logging operations with two or three men on a float camp to the giants where there might be hundreds of loggers, mechanics, welders, cooks, bull cooks and sometimes even wives and families as was the case up at Woss Camp where I hung my hat during the week.

After a night of rain and wind I should have known better than to set out to cross the strait next morning. Hindsight is a grand tool.

I try to avoid exaggeration in this account but this time it is difficult to play down my predicament when, on a lee shore with waves breaking on the rocks of each headland, I claw my way up close to the island. I would very much like to retreat to Beaver Cove, but there is no chance in the world that I could make headway against the south wind that blows fiercely up the strait.

Goodness only knows what would have happened to me, but I have a strong suspicion that it could have been decidedly sticky if providence had not arranged for a sheltered cove with a marina exactly where I had need of them. There was nothing like this forty years ago, and I have seen no sign of it on my chart which admittedly is about ten years out of date.

I shoot inside the protecting arms of the cove. It has been a close call. My guardian angel has been working overtime.

A smiling man drinks from a mug at the taffrail of a cabin cruiser registered in Bellingham, Washington State.

"A stormy day," he says.

"Indeed," say I. I could say a good deal more but I am still catching my breath.

"Spending the night here?" he asks.

"I may have to though I'd rather not. I want to get across to Alert Bay today."

He is an affable fellow on a fishing trip, and we chat of this and that and generally put the world in perspective and in its proper place for an hour or two. Finally, my new friend says:

"You know, I think it's getting a bit calmer out there. Take a look and see what you think." My back is to the mouth of the bay, intentionally shutting off all sight of the horrors of the strait, I guess.

When you are as keen as I am to get across a small stretch of water you can convince yourself of almost anything and, anyway, it does seem that the waves are less and the trees at the mouth of the cove are not swaying and bending as much as they had been when I gasped my way inside a couple of hours ago.

"Tell you what," says the American, "I'll watch you go. If it looks like you're in trouble I'll come out to help."

This is kindness indeed and an offer I can't turn down.

It proves a stiff enough pull to cross the strait, but everything is better than it had been when I thought I was the luckiest man alive to find the cove, the marina and my friendly American. I'm not usually in the business of counting my chickens before they are hatched, but I really think I have made it over successfully when I am almost within shouting distance of the first of the Alert Bay wharves. But I find myself suddenly in the grip of a fierce tidal current. I have no idea how strong it is in terms of knots; all I can say is that I am powerless to beat it with my oars. The boat is swirled out from land and taken quickly towards the rocky point at the far end of the bay where, as I remember, quite a few boats have come to grief.

It is a grim prospect.

The best I can do is try to save myself if we strike. This will not be easy and, as for saving the boat, that is out of the question. I am struggling into my life jacket when I happen to glance astern and there, by George, is my American friend cruising a watching brief, not a quarter of a mile away. Talk about the U.S. Marines coming to the rescue with bugles blowing; they don't have a look-in. I stand up, oar in hand and wave, the international signal of distress for a small boat. By the size of his bow wave I can tell he is giving his motor full throttle as soon as he sees the pickle I am in.

It is a near thing. I throw a line and his crewman makes it fast. We are almost within touching distance of the rocks. Another two or three minutes would have seen the end of *Morag Anne* and perhaps me as well. At full ahead he fights against the current, making very little headway for what seems an agonisingly long time. Slowly, slowly however we escape from the grip of the tide.

He casts me loose at the breakwater.

"There you go," is his laconic farewell as I retrieve my line and before I know it, he is pulling away. I barely have time to shout, "His name, what's the skipper's name?"

"Dan Flynn," comes the answer and they are gone.

To my everlasting regret I have not been able to track down Dan Flynn and thank him. I'll keep on trying.

I find moorage at the crowded wharf inside a new breakwater. As usual, it is a case of "That's a pretty little boat you've got" and in no time a small crowd gathers. They watch me make breakfast. There is no privacy in a small open boat.

Quite a little parliament assembles. Most of them sit on an upturned dinghy while others lean against a pile of nets.

One of the members of this group of interested fishermen, cruisers and Alert Bay citizens is a heavily bearded, bespectacled young man with a twinkling brown eye who is addressed by everyone as Bughouse, or Bughouse Bill. I learn that he is a sometime caretaker of a logging camp in Bughouse Bay. He doesn't appear to mind his name and he takes me aside when I am finished eating.

"Look," he says, "you really didn't ought to go farther up the strait." He means Queen Charlotte Strait for I have been asking questions about Cape Caution which you must pass in order to get into Queen Charlotte Sound. "Cape Caution is a killer. Anyhow, you've got nothing to prove. You've shown yourself you can row. Whyn't you have some fun around these parts before you go back to Vancouver?"

By fun Bughouse means exploring the archipelago around the eastern end of the strait. As an added inducement to stray from my original plan, he adds, "There's a hootenanny over at Echo Bay in a couple of nights. The teacher's quittin' and they're putting on a dance for her. I'll be there and so will most everybody that has a boat around here."

I tell him I will certainly think about it.

A more immediate concern is to find somewhere to spend the night ashore. I don't fancy putting the tent up and sleeping quite so exposed to the public and in any case at full ebb *Morag Anne* might very well find herself sitting on the mud. Anyway, I feel rather dirty and the thought of a shower and a night between clean sheets is pretty well irresistible.

The Orca Hotel gives me an excellent room but I can't say I sleep very well. The room heaves and rolls all night, the result of being too many nights rocked gently to sleep by *Morag Anne.*

Rain comes down in torrents all the next day. I row the boat around to the old government wharf, the same wharf that the *Camosun* brought me to in 1951. This is deep water. I am able to put up the tent and in spite of the rain, spend a pleasant night after a gargantuan meal of fish and chips with old friends.

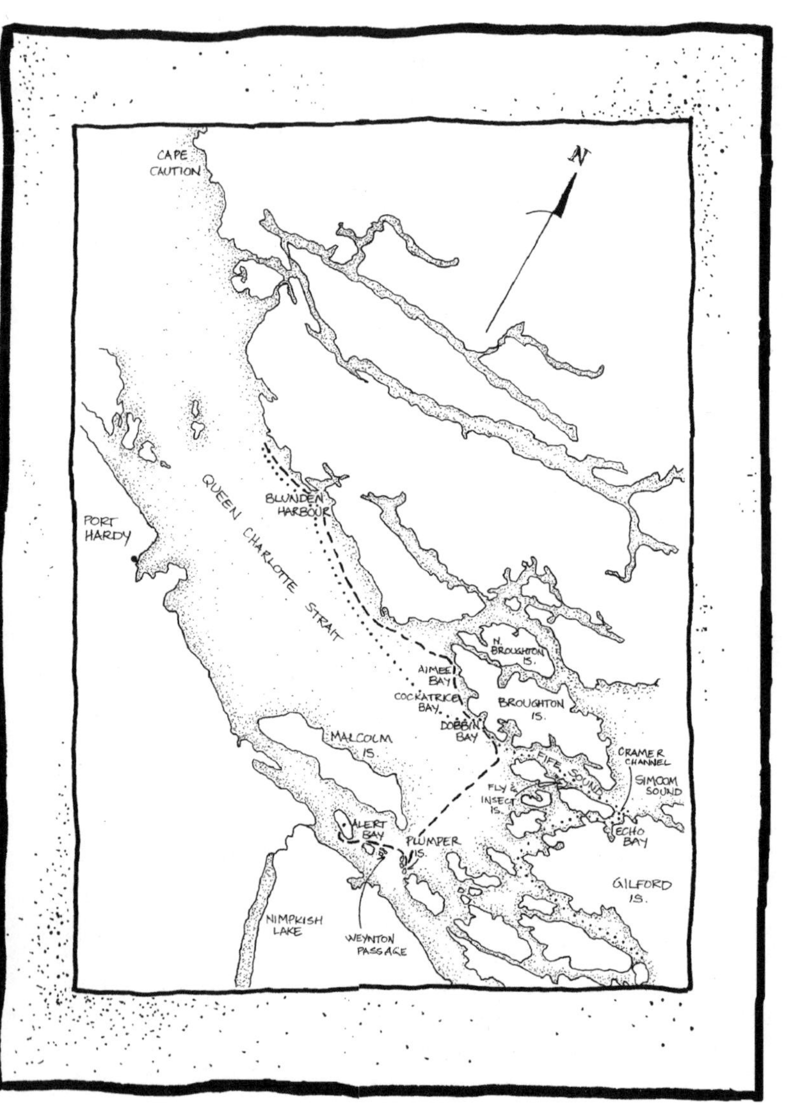
N
CAPE CAUTION
PORT HARDY
QUEEN CHARLOTTE STRAIT
BLUNDEN HARBOUR
N. BROUGHTON IS.
AIMEE BAY
COCKATRICE BAY
BROUGHTON IS.
DOBBIN BAY
MALCOLM IS.
FIFE SOUND
CRAMER CHANNEL
SIMOOM SOUND
FLY & INSECT IS.
ECHO BAY
ALERT BAY
PLUMPER IS.
GILFORD IS.
NIMPKISH LAKE
WEYNTON PASSAGE

Chapter Five

The better part of valor is discretion.
Shakespeare, HENRY IV

I AM A genuine and proud Canadian and have thus mastered the art of compromise. Therefore, still undecided whether to abandon the goal of Prince Rupert and to cruise these waters or to get my head down and make for Cape Caution and beyond, I decide to cruise a bit and, at the same time, head more or less in the direction of Cape Caution and see what happens.

A day of sunshine which takes me to Plumper Islands in Weynton Passage is followed by another of heavy rain, fog, mist and such warmth that rowing in foul weather gear is purgatory relieved only a little by a world of seals and sea lions. The latter bob up beside *Morag Anne* eyeing me mournfully, bald pates moistly sleek and freckled.

I spend the night in what I think is Aimee Bay but cannot be certain because I have had little opportunity to check my chart during the day. A couple of minutes in that downpour would turn my charts to pulp.

I try crawling under the foredeck. This in itself, in Helly Hansen pants and jacket, is no mean feat. The opened chart, folded and refolded, can be held no further than a couple of inches from my eyes, much too close for clarity, spectacles notwithstanding.

When I get up the tent, sponge the wet deck and towel it dry, I am able to spread out the chart for the first time. I note that Aimee Bay, if this is Aimee Bay, lies just beyond

Cockatrice Bay. Now, everyone knows the cockatrice, don't they? Well, not I. I have to wait until this adventure is over to discover it has nothing to do with the farmyard.

Chambers Dictionary, my indefatigable guide, tells me it is "a mythical beast resembling a basilisk". This isn't a great help for, apart from a basilisk stare, I know as much of the basilisk as the cockatrice. Back to *Chambers*. The basilisk, also mythical, is "serpent-like" and able to kill by a glance or even by breathing on its victim.

Next morning everything seems right. The sun shines, there is a breeze — a little breeze to be sure but still more than a zephyr — blowing westward. The tide is flowing in the same direction and oh, I can't tell exactly what it is, but every omen and portent appears to point towards Rupert. So it is westward ho for me.

On second thought, it isn't. Westward ho I mean. I should remember Hilaire Belloc's words:

> *'Westward Ho' which Kingsley rendered famous. Westward ho simply means the westerly of two landing places. Ho or hoe is a wharf. But, that 'Ho' has been spread throughout the world of English as a sort of 'Hulloa' or 'Yoiks' to call the adventurous overseas.*

How could I have forgotten Newbolt's *Drake's Drum* where Drake was "slung atween the round shot in Nombre Dios Bay, An' dreamin' arl the time o' Plymouth Hoe"? Foolish me.

So, not "westward ho" but simply "westward."

The northern shore of Queen Charlotte Strait is a lonesome stretch. I meet no one, see no one and surprisingly, hear no aircraft as I row and, later, sail into the little archipelago of islands that shields the entrance to Blunden Harbour where I arrive in the evening gloaming.

Blunden Harbour is entrancingly described by Wylie Blanchet in *The Curve of Time.* To see it for myself is definitely one of the ambitions of this voyage. Getting there is the fulfillment of a dream.

The small islands in this part of the strait are delightful. I dare say in stormy weather they would be less appealing. I meet them at dusk, in calm weather, the western sky aglow, salmon-coloured clouds radiating from the horizon. Add to this that I am primed by Blanchet to expect wonderment. Atmosphere and ambiance are all and everything to me.

Some of the islands are so small that only a couple of trees stand on a rocky platform above a kelp-fringed shore or a little beach of silver sand. The water is a clear shimmering green as I look into the depths. Every island beckons but, in the grip of determination to "get on", I ignore the call. Some day, perhaps, I'll be lucky enough to see them again. For the moment I can say I know what paradise looks like.

I have few regrets about my voyage, adventure, odyssey, call it what you will. But, as I write, I can see a constant error threading its way throughout. The goal appears to have been everything. This is foolish and very short-sighted. But retrospection never does anybody any good. I must live with my mistake.

I can say that I have the wisdom to recognize my luck when I meet *Taku Flicka,* a thirty-foot yacht, nosing out from Blunden Harbour with a greybeard at the helm and a crew of gorgeous girls, long-limbed and blonde, not surprising on a boat with a Swedish name I guess. Flicka is girl in Swedish. Do I ogle, I wonder? If elderly oarsmen can ogle then I guess I do.

"Is this Blunden Harbour?" I ask, for I can see no harbour.

"It sure is," says the skipper. "Don't you have a chart?"

There is a chart across my knees but politeness forbids me to draw this to his attention.

Taku Flicka, with her magnificent crew, slides away into the gathering dusk and I enter a deserted Blunden Harbour, drop the anchor in a tiny bay where every tall cedar seems to have an eagle and marvel at the peace and tranquillity of the beautiful place.

Indians used to bury their dead here, placing the corpse in a tree. If I did not already know this, I think I would still feel there is something special about the harbour, its silver beach of crushed shell, the dark, sombre cedars and the silence.

Next morning everything is more silent, positively sepulchral in fact. Thick fog is everywhere, so thick that I cannot see the shore. The canvas of the tent is as wet as if it had rained all night and everything on the boat is pearled with dew, including the sleeping bag.

When there is a fog like this there can be no wind. If I could catch the tide I might make good progress towards Cape Caution.

Leaving the bay, rowing is easy but I am forced, by fog and mist, to follow the shoreline, catching glimpses of the beach from time to time and keeping an ear open for the sound of breakers. There can be no cutting across a bay if I am to keep a steady course.

After several hours of this I feel a faint breeze. Slowly the fog begins to thin and finally clear completely. But alas, the wind is from the west and as it freshens the direction of the tidal current changes. The Pacific, uninterrupted from Japan, is more than I can handle.

Then, a very strange thing happens. I am pulling hard on the oars, rising a little from the cushion with each stroke when suddenly, without any warning, a filling pops out of a molar. Just like that.

I am no more superstitious than the next man; born on a thirteenth day I may be less superstitious than most. First fog, then the wind and tide against me and now this. If ever, I say to myself, if ever there was an omen, this surely is it. Anyway, it is clear that not only am I not making headway, I am losing ground. As I sit and explore the cavity with my tongue, I can see by the shoreline that the boat is moving backwards. I turn around and retreat towards Blunden Harbour.

Even as I do this, I realize it is a portentous move. I know that I am not going to make another attempt to round Cape Caution. Time and food are running low. Once around the cape there will be no supplies until Namu or even Bella Bella. But I must tell the truth; I am also lonely and, yes, dispirited. The strait is wide at that point. The Pacific swell is no danger but a monotonous, forceful reminder of the strength of the ocean. Like the ancient mariner of Coleridge I feel very much

Alone, alone, all, all alone,
Alone on a wide, wide sea!

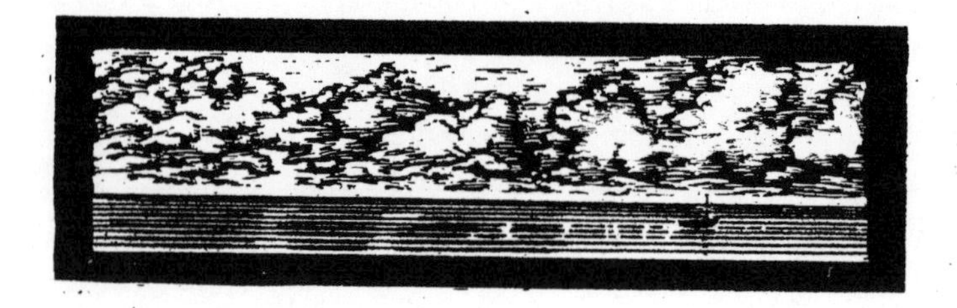

The sun comes out, I raise sail and scud home. My spirits rise. Gloom is dispelled. With wind and tide in my favour I am back in less than three hours, covering the same distance that had earlier required six or more. Blunden Harbour is once more a pleasant refuge. This time there is another boat, a cabin cruiser at anchor at the head of the bay. Humankind must have brought her there but I see neither hide nor hair of them and by morning she is gone. She must have slid by me very silently for I am anchored close to the narrow entrance to the harbour.

The sun is shining when I wake. My tiny receiver is able to pull in Alert Bay Coast Guard. I am pleased to hear "strong winds are expected in Queen Charlotte Sound, at times reaching hurricane force." Serendipitously, the retreat to Blunden Harbour was the right move. Hurricane force winds. No thanks.

I row out of the harbour, saying *au revoir*, raise both sails and speed down the strait on a beautiful beam reach enjoying what is possibly the best sailing day of the entire adventure.

Queen Charlotte's name is attached to a strait, a sound and the westernmost islands. Poor Queen Charlotte, she certainly had a cross to bear in the shape of the intermittent madness of her husband, George the Third. Not that he is any less deserving of our sympathy. His madness was probably due to porphyria, an hereditary disease that came to him by way of Mary Queen of Scots, but I won't go into that. Anyway, there is no end of Georgias to commemorate him. It is only fitting that his consort got her name on the map as well.

A glorious day indeed, and a glorious sail. But eventually the wind dies away as winds will, and the flood turns to ebb, flowing against me. So it is out with the oars and a good stiff pull to Dobbin Bay, still on Queen Charlotte Strait. Here I have to confess something. I am as happy as the next man to sit in the sternsheets with the tiller under my arm as the boat scuds along, sails drawing well and the wake thrumming against the rudder. But not for too long, and certainly not for all day. I guess I am just not a real sailorman. I need to feel I am doing something positive to contribute to the passage, something other than merely pointing the boat in the right direction. Therefore I'm not particularly put out when I have to work and work quite hard to gain the entrance to the bay where two eagles sit on a guardian rock and watch as I inch past, the strong ebb swirling the nut-brown sea-wrack at their feet.

Colonel John Joseph O'Sullivan, whom God and the saints preserve, long ago in the desert of Cyrenaica imprinted on me the maxim that "any fool can be uncomfortable." I mention this to introduce the topic of cushions. To my mind, anyone who goes rowing for more than a couple of hours without a cushion between his fundament and the thwart is a masochist and I have no time for masochists. A thick foam rubber pad makes a good enough cushion but it has one drawback — well, one and a half as a matter of fact. The half drawback is the fact that even the best and thickest pad does compress to become pretty thin. There isn't much you can do about that. Much more serious is what happens when it is repeatedly sat upon while it is sodden. As I discovered somewhere about Dobbin Bay, the cushion crumbles and begins to feel like ball bearings or lead shot. All this in spite of wrapping the pad in a stout plastic garbage bag, liberally bound with duct tape, for even the stoutest bag manages to get itself punctured over the course of a week or two of cruising.

In Dobbin Bay and thereafter there wasn't a thing to be done about this. The subject of cushions is now closed. I'm sorry, in a way, I ever mentioned it.

Masts by their very nature sit vertically on a boat. When it rains, water runs down them. This is a constant headache for the yachtsman and never more so than for the yachtsman who must build his tent afresh each night around his mast. Any small boat sailor who suffers or has suffered the annoyance of a wet, soggy pillow or sleeping bag should pay heed to what I have to tell him or her. This advice I give freely and cheerfully for it is the fruit of bitter experience. Your mast, beneath the point of attachment of your tent, can be kept absolutely dry if you will wrap a plastic shopping bag around the outside and hold it tightly against the tent with two separate elastic shock cords wound as tightly as possible around the outside of the bag.

The non-sailor or even the big boat sailor will say, "Ho hum," but the open boat cruiser who hasn't discovered this dodge for himself should and possibly will bless me for this information. The idea came to me in Dobbin Bay and I think the bags deserve to be known as "Dobbin Bay bags".

Next day I reach Echo Bay. I think I am going to Simoom Sound for that's certainly what the chart seems to say, but as I row into the bay, there is a sign that clearly says Echo Bay Marina together with another that reads Simoom Sound Post Office. Even the most unexpected phenomenon generally has an explanation, and in this case the answer to the apparent conundrum is that Simoom Sound simply folded up as a settlement when logging came to an end there. The post office was moved a few miles to Echo Bay. No one, it seems, has got around to changing its name. If you are in the know, and even if you aren't I suppose, it doesn't really matter.

Rowing up Fife Sound towards Echo Bay I pass Fly and Insect Islands, and both of them are well named for I am pestered by hordes of strange-looking flies with grey spots on their backs. I don't know who gave names to the islands and I don't suppose he was rowing when he did, otherwise he would have thrown in an adjective or two along with the bare nouns. When finally they leave me alone, I am most relieved and moderately sure that nothing the rest of the day has in store will be half so aggravating, and so more or less it proves. The one possible exception comes when I am struggling, really struggling, to cross Cramer Channel over to Echo Bay in the teeth of a strong wind and choppy sea. About half a dozen boats are heading in the same direction and, I suppose, for the same reason, namely that dirty weather is coming. Every single one of them passes within hail of *Morag Anne* and not a mother's son among them offers a tow or help, and there I am, standing up at each oar-stroke and pulling till I think I will burst. Any other time, every Tom, Dick and Harry would have slowed down to say "That's a pretty little boat." Fate, I suppose, perverse fate.

Of all strange things, well it seems strange to me at any rate, what is there, right inside Echo Bay on a float, but an art gallery? It is too much to pass something so unexpected so I moor to the float and go inside. What I find is what I call proper art, that is to say paintings of things, and good paintings that I can understand. All coastal scenes, most attractively done, all of them as far as I recall, watercolours. Not a simple medium in which to excel. The pleasant woman who seems to be in charge tells me she was born in Alert Bay which, naturally, at once establishes a mutual bond between us and I spend far too much time bending her ear with reminiscence.

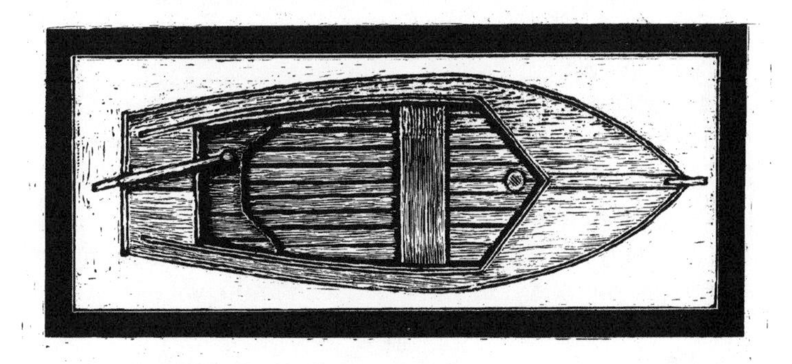

The wind howls and trumpets in Cramer Channel and nasty looking waves crest at the entrance to the bay but inside all is peaceful. I anchor at the head of the bay, near the schoolhouse as a matter of fact, the site, I guess, of Bughouse Bill's hootenanny, now nothing more than a memory.

On the other side of the bay, on another float, is the combined store and post office. I make it sound, perhaps, as if this is quite a distance but in fact you could almost spit across. I row there. A sign says Government Liquor Store. A thought comes quickly to mind.

Behind the counter stands a woman who is eating an iced bun.

"How did you get here? I didn't hear you come into the bay."

"I rowed."

"Hmph. Somethin' wrong with your motor?"

"No, I don't have one."

"Hmph. Can't anchor anywhere near here. There's boats comin' in an' out all night."

Well, say I to myself, reverting to the thought that had sprung to mind when I saw the liquor store sign, I'll celebrate nothing in particular with a bottle of beer.

"We don't sell by the bottle. It's a dozen or nothin'."

Hmph, yourself then, think I, for I am dashed if I want to lug a dozen bottles, full or empty, in the bilge where I store anything that is best kept cold.

The woman is dead right about the boats; although, once the marina is full and this doesn't take very long, no more come in. I suppose they see from the mouth of the bay there is no room and push on to somewhere else. However, the night is loud with the humming and throbbing of the generators of the vessels tied to the wharf. Most of them are very big boats and big boats, it appears, can't support life without a generator. On such a night, I find ear plugs a blessing and a boon.

Readers of my generation will recognize that I have those nouns the wrong way around.

> *They came as a boon and a blessing to men,*
> *The Pickwick, the Owl and the Waverley pen.*

So said the tin signs in railway stations along with advertisements for Mazawatee Tea and Fry's Chocolate in those dear dead days when the London, Midland and

Scottish Railway plied its punctual tracks and the Flying Scot flew on time from London to Edinburgh at more than a hundred almost unbelievable miles an hour.

I am away next morning before curtains are pulled on the mini-liners, almost all of them flying the Stars and Stripes. A heavy-eyed matron wearing a pink pantsuit leads a miniature white dog along the wharf for its matutinal business.

Farewell Echo Bay, alias Simoom Sound.

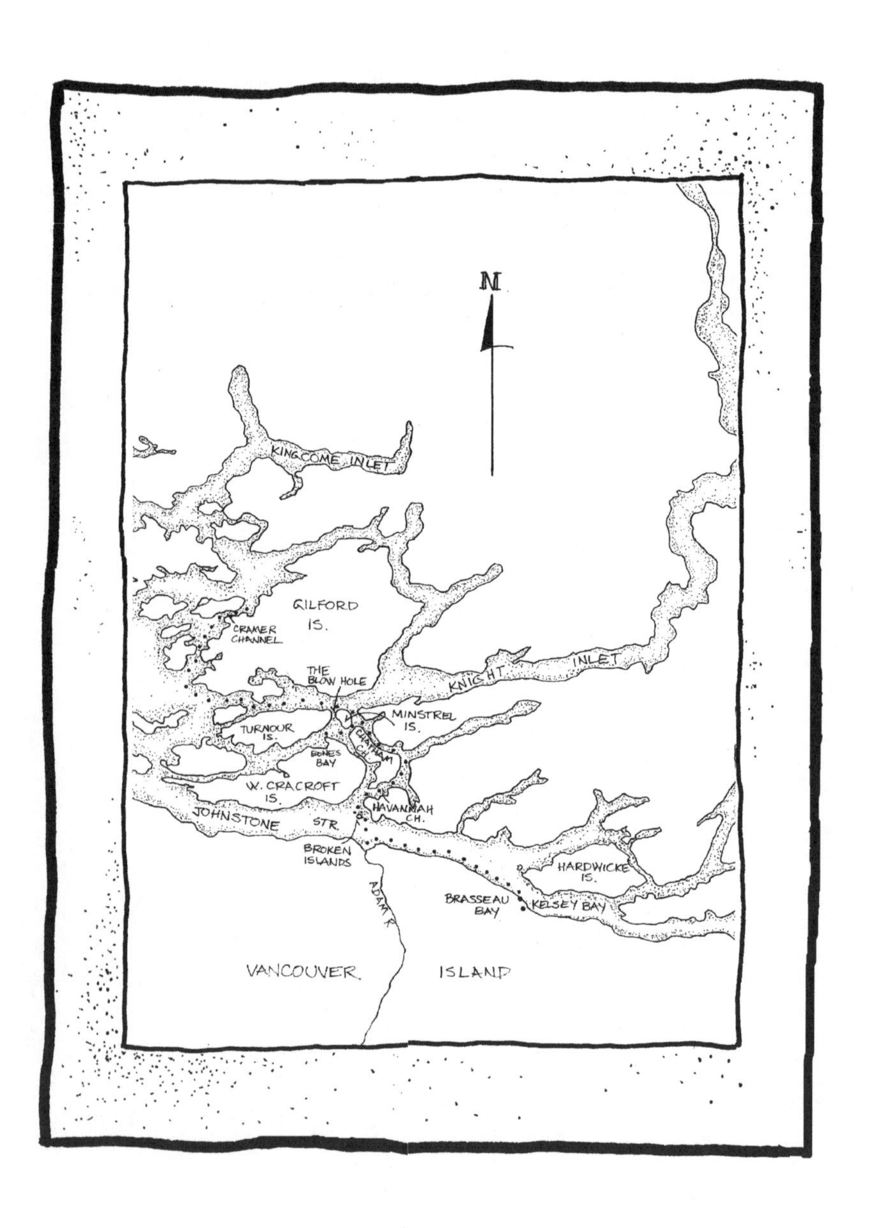
N
KINGCOME INLET
GILFORD IS.
CRAMER CHANNEL
THE BLOW HOLE
KNIGHT INLET
MINSTREL IS.
TURNOUR IS.
BONES BAY
CHATHAM CH.
W. CRACROFT IS.
HAVANNAH CH.
JOHNSTONE STR.
BROKEN ISLANDS
ADAM R.
HARDWICKE IS.
BRASSEAU BAY
KELSEY BAY
VANCOUVER ISLAND

Chapter Six

... and we decided before we slept that it was better never to reason upon tides, nor even to accept print upon them, but to take them blindly as they came, for no man living can understand the tides ...

Hilaire Belloc,
THE CRUISE OF THE NONA

I SEE A magnificent sight as I row down Cramer Passage in the morning sunshine. Craning my neck over my shoulder to pick a passage amongst a host of islands, I catch a glimpse of a big, bottle-green yacht and turn *Morag Anne* to watch her fly across my course, well heeled to the wind, canvas taut, bright-work sparkling, ship's bell gleaming and the Canadian Ensign stiff and proud over her stern. A bearded man at the wheel, looking like Joseph Conrad or Jules Verne's Captain Nemo, responds gravely to my wave. I wish I had a flag of my own to dip in courtesy and appreciation.

This is a good omen for a good day that is interrupted by only one bizarre accident I am almost ashamed to mention. I manage, by a feat of contortionism that would be impossible to repeat if ever I wanted to, which is unlikely, to stab myself in the flank with the fluke of the anchor. I fall to the deck winded, sore and mortified and lie recovering for quite a while as *Morag Anne*, sensible craft, looks after herself in a freshening breeze. I won't describe the accident. The anchor sits in a bucket at the mast foot. I tripped. And that's enough of that.

This contretemps apart, I enjoy a row and sail into and up Knight Inlet to a fine, wide bay on Gilford Island. Here I spend the night, first stranding the boat on a rising tide where a stream comes down a wide curving sandy beach from the ruins of an ancient forest, long ago logged and devastated.

I fill a container with fresh water and retire to mid-bay to anchor and listen only to the murmur of the stream, the cry of gulls and the splash and plop of several porpoises, friendly creatures who do not object to the presence of an intruder.

By noon the following day I am at Minstrel Island. Turnour Island comes first, separated from Minstrel by a passage called The Blow Hole. This name has no appeal and I therefore give it a wide berth, quite mistakenly it turns out, but with a name like that and in a small open boat it pays to be cautious.

Turnour, after whom the island is named, interests me greatly. Walbran, in his inestimable *British Columbia Coast Names*, tells me that he was "shot through the body" in 1848 while storming Fort Serapequi in Nicaragua as a midshipman in the Royal Navy. Anyone who survived such a wound in 1848 was a very lucky man indeed but what, I ask myself, was the Royal Navy doing ashore in Nicaragua that year? I shall find out someday.

Minstrel is believed to get its name from a travelling concert party which is as likely a story as any. I visit the store and the hotel, buying some sweet biscuits at the former and enjoying a shower in the latter. The shower, although most welcome, has to be very brief for the island is in the grip of a water shortage, not a common occurrence on this coast.

Chatham Channel connects Knight Inlet with Johnstone Strait. I wait in a small bay, out of sight of the hotel guests, brew tea and eat my biscuits, and at slack water, before the start of the flood tide, set off down the channel.

The rain starts almost as soon as I set off. It is heavy enough to make me put on foul weather gear and I battle on. Little by little I find it is a much stiffer pull than I feel it should be. Pretty soon I'm not making any headway whatsoever. But this is not possible. The arrows on my chart show quite clearly that the flood tide runs from Knight to Johnstone, and my tables tell me the flood is well under way. At first I think I am in a back eddy and make for mid-channel. Conditions there are a good deal worse. When I get back to the side, I can keep my position only by clinging to a strand of slippery kelp.

The rain is torrential by this time, mist and cloud shroud a dismal scene. My spirits sink.

On my way down Chatham Channel from Minstrel, before the going got tough, I passed a decrepit wharf, tip-tilted and crumbling on the opposite bank. On this wharf was a sign which read Minstrel Island Post Office; this was indeed strange for Minstrel was a good two miles upstream.

Also, there were no buildings or any other sign of life, nothing but the impenetrable forest.

As soon as I let go of the kelp I am instantly swept back upstream. As I swirl past the deserted wharf I contrive to pass close enough to grab an old car tire dangling over the side. I tie up *Morag Anne* and stand on the wharf, on the other side of which I now see an aluminum run-about with a canvas cover and small outboard motor.

By this time it is raining more than ever. I am wet, cold, miserable and bewildered. Indeed I am on the point of boarding *Morag Anne* once more and accepting a rapid return to Minstrel when a figure emerges from the forest in glistening oilskins, sou'wester and sea boots. I wait and presently a young man joins me. He is, it appears, a man of few words. Not that this matters, I would have embraced him had he been deaf and dumb.

"Trouble?" he asks.

"Yes, indeed," I begin, but he cuts me short.

"Better come with me," and leads off up a dripping, slippery cedar log with two or three notches cut for footholds and into the dark forest along a narrow muddy track.

Presently we arrive at a clearing where, to my surprise, sits a mobile home. I don't ask how it got there; certainly I can see no road. My rescuer leads me up steps to the door which is opened by a pleasant-looking woman who says, "Hi. I'm Pat Davidson, the postmistress. Come on in. Drop your wet things, come sit by the stove. Would you like some tea or coffee?"

Wouldn't I just.

Later, toasting stocking feet at the wood stove, listening to rain bouncing on the metal roof, I learn about the tides in Chatham Channel from Derick, my rescuer.

"You see," he says, "the flood comes down both Knight and Johnstone. From Knight it comes through Chatham which you can see is pretty narrow whereas Johnstone is wide. So she comes stronger down Johnstone at the start. She only comes down Chatham once she's slackening in Johnstone which is about two or three hours after the start of the flood. Up to then she's coming up Chatham, the wrong way you could say, like an express train."

I can vouch for the last part.

We chat most amicably, I eat biscuits and buns, drink tea and dry my wet socks and sweaters and listen to the rain which doesn't sound as if it is ever going to stop. When Derick offers to tow *Morag Anne* down to Bones Bay I jump at the chance. Who wouldn't?

We battle downstream with *Morag Anne* bobbing and tugging at her line behind the run-about where, under the canvas cover, Derick and I are comfortably dry. He is a deep-sea diver by trade, and just as surprising to me although there is really no reason why it should be, so is his father.

"What, in the name of heaven," I ask, "is a deep-sea diver doing in Chatham Sound?"

"I'm as busy as heck," he says, "untangling the mess when these fish-boat skippers back their boats over their own nets and get them all fouled up in the screw."

"Do they do this often?"

"All the time."

Derick drops me at the entrance to Bones Bay which is on the north side of West Cracroft Island. Bones Bay is big enough to take the Grand Fleet but there are only two other boats at anchor, and as luck would have it, I misjudge things and drop my hook rather closer than is polite to a nice looking yacht which is registered in Phoenix, Arizona.

I don't notice how close I am until I have the tent up and the inside of the boat pretty well dried out with sponge and towel. I am eyeing *Dulcinea,* my too close companion from the United States and thinking I really should move when a head appears at her side.

"Are you all right?"

"Yes, thanks. My apologies for mooring so close. I hope you don't mind."

"Not a bit. My wife and I would like you to come over and eat with us. I'll fetch you in my dinghy."

Some days you just strike it lucky.

It doesn't seem right to go across to such a spick and span boat looking like a Newfoundland fisherman, an advertisement for cod-liver oil in oilskins, sou'wester and sea boots, so I make a quick change into shorts, socks and running shoes much to the consternation of the skipper's wife who greets me as I come over the side of her boat.

"Land sakes, is that all you wear in weather like this? Look at you. You're all covered in goose bumps. Come below right this very minute. Sit down and have some hot coffee and, here, take an oatmeal cookie, it's fresh out of the oven."

Something we used to say when we were particularly satisfied with life was, "I wouldn't call the king my uncle." That's how I am for the rest of a memorable evening. I feast in a warm, snug cabin, talk too much and revel in genuine American hospitality of which, let me tell you, there is no finer. To top it all off, my hostess presses upon me the remainder of the oatmeal cookies as I leave.

"Take them with you. If you don't, we'll only eat them and we need them like a hole in the head. I like to see a man with a good appetite."

Next day I am lucky enough to catch Len McPhee just as he is about to set off in his tug. He has a house, a most elegant Japanese-style house, on the shore of Bones Bay. Derick has spoken to me about him, telling me that I should ask him about the tides in Chatham.

Mrs. McPhee is on the wharf to see her husband leave, a youngster at her side. She is Japanese-Canadian which may account for the architecture of the delightful house. She invites me for breakfast and, ever ready for a meal, I am on the point of accepting when Len says, "If you set off now, you'll catch the tide and be down in Johnstone Strait in jig time. Wait an hour and you'll wait twelve."

So, no breakfast, just a hasty farewell and pull as hard as possible for the channel of Chatham.

Local knowledge is once again the key to success. Jig time it isn't but I can't blame Len McPhee. Not many people remember the speed of a rowing boat. No matter, I am at anchor behind the Broken Islands in Johnstone Strait by the late afternoon after a glorious row in calm water with a following tide most of the way.

The Broken Islands are surrounded by kelp so I'm not terribly enthusiastic about anchoring there. It's easy enough to get a good firm hold on the bottom and there is never a chance that the anchor will drag but the problem comes when you want to get it up again for kelp has an uncanny knack of insinuating itself around and through the chain, around and around the warp from chain to boat and even between rudder and hull. However, beggars can't be choosers. The alternative is to row across the strait to the Vancouver Island shore and that is just too far.

A good night, not a great deal of trouble getting up the anchor in the morning, but a major concern with the thick fog that I find surrounding *Morag Anne* as soon as I move from the shelter of the island. This is hairy, to put it mildly, for the strait is a busy thoroughfare and no place for a small boat in thick fog, invisible to radar and incapable of quickly escaping the path of a vessel suddenly encountered in mid-stream. Not that there is anything to be done about it but set the compass direction, align the bow with the needle, and keeping it there, row as hard as possible, both ears cocked for the sound of engines while praying I won't hear any.

I almost run ashore on the beach of the island before seeing it, but after I turn south, the fog lifts with a breeze which shortly blows so hard that I am forced into the bay of the Adam River. I eat a second breakfast. At first I am moored to an enormous log boom which looks as if it has been there since the beginning of time and is likely to stay forever but onto which descends a team of men with pike poles and peavies and before you can say knife, they untie chains, hook up a couple of tugs and send her on her way across the strait at a slow, sedate pace ignoring the fresh southeast wind.

Ignoring the wind is something I wish I could do. I struggle across the mouth of the Adam River for what seems an age and possibly is. It is necessary to zig and zag to make headway and when I finally get to the south side I have to hug close to the shore, following every indentation and hiding behind each headland for some protection from the wind.

"I'll take anything but this," I think to myself, but these are words I come to regret for, around mid-day, the wind dies completely, the sun beats from a cloudless sky and all the energy seems to drip away from my limbs. Unfortunately the shore offers nothing much in the way of an anchorage for the night. If anything half worthwhile would appear I would take it like a shot. As a matter of fact, and it's in the nature of things, I am lucky I don't find anything for, out of the blue, what should appear but Mike Sacht's boat.

"Have you had your breakfast?"

Of course breakfast is just a memory and this doesn't prevent me from going aboard, out there in the middle of the strait, and enjoying the freshest salmon steaks in the whole wide world, fried bread and coffee and Mrs. Mike to cook and mollycoddle me.

Just call me a lucky man.

Later on, alone once more on the burning sea and getting thoroughly fed up with myself, I hitch a tow with a whale-watching boat that is on its way back to Kelsey Bay with a load of tourists. They tow me the last five miles or so and I am immensely glad for their help. And for their hospitality.

"Go into the cabin and help yourself," says the skipper after I climb over the transom. "There's all sorts of grub there and it doesn't look as if this lot is going to do a whole lot about it."

"This lot" are mostly Japanese, very young Japanese, it seems, and they are disposed on every bench and chair, sound asleep. The very few who aren't snoozing are playing chess and oblivious to the spread in the saloon and the magnificent coastal scenery passing unseen outside.

I make short work of a good proportion of the sandwiches, cake and soft drinks and then, when killer whales start to sport, like good British Columbians, alongside the vessel, I can do no less than waken the somnolent orientals and encourage them to see what they had paid for.

They come on deck, reluctantly and yawning sleepily. Once outside in the sunshine, they line each other against the railing, facing inboard away from the scenery and the whales. Then all take photographs of their neighbours.

I detach myself from the whale-watchers at the entrance to Brasseau Bay, with hearty thanks to the friendly skipper and his crew. I guess it is all one to them what the paying customers do with their time on the not inexpensive trip.

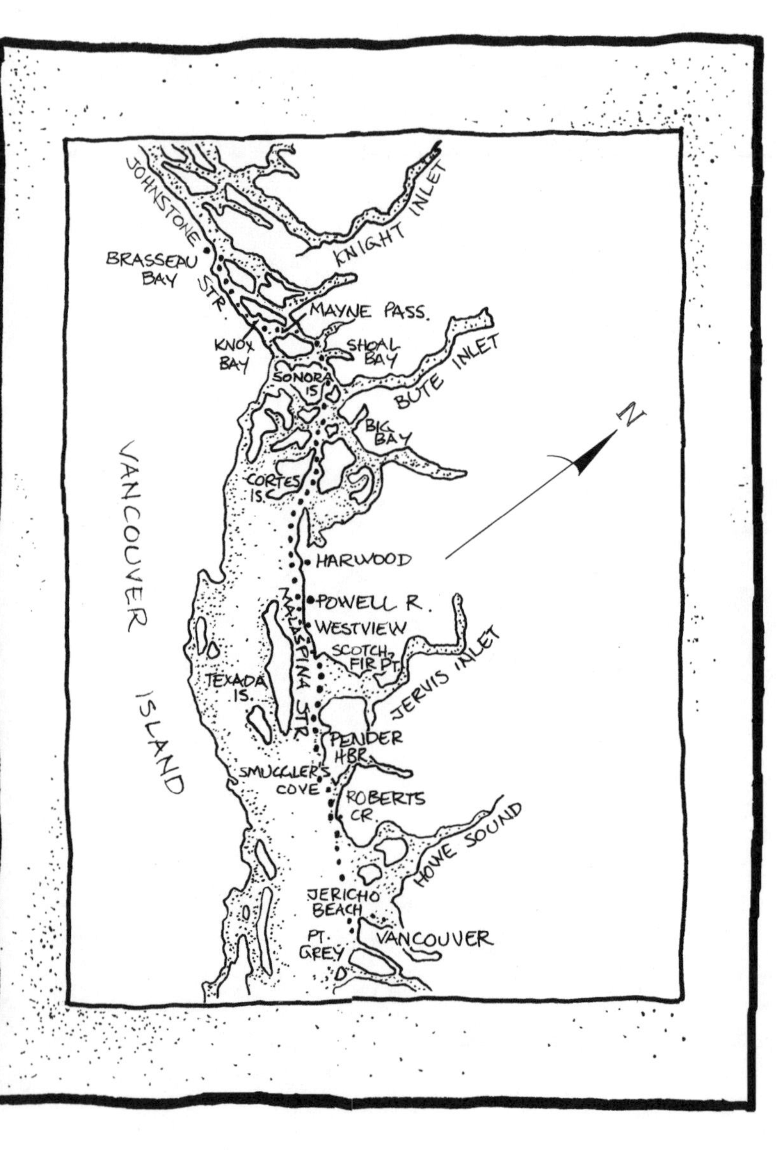
JOHNSTONE STR.
KNIGHT INLET
BRASSEAU BAY
MAYNE PASS.
KNOX BAY
SHOAL BAY
SONORA IS.
BUTE INLET
BIG BAY
N
VANCOUVER ISLAND
CORTES IS.
HARWOOD
POWELL R.
WESTVIEW
MALASPINA STR.
SCOTCH FIR PT.
JERVIS INLET
TEXADA IS.
PENDER HBR.
SMUGGLER'S COVE
ROBERTS CR.
HOWE SOUND
JERICHO BEACH
PT. GREY
VANCOUVER

Chapter Seven

Le secret d'ennuyer est ... de tout dire.
(The way to be a bore is to say everything.)
Voltaire

TO BEAR in mind Voltaire's admonition, let me simply say that Brasseau Bay is pleasant, the honeysuckle is still in bloom and Mr. Fred's welcome as warm as ever.

The big event next morning as I row down Johnstone Strait is meeting a tidal wave, also known as a tidal bore. No one warns me this is a possibility. The first I know of it is the sound. When I look over my shoulder all I can see is a wall of water, about four feet high, coming steadily up the strait. There is nothing I can do about it. The wave stretches from one shore to the other. I cannot see what lies behind the wave so I point the bow straight at it and hope for the best.

For a second or two it is quite exciting. The sea behind the wave is thoroughly confused and broken, but once through that, all is calm. I watch a yacht that follows under power toss about with a clanging of shrouds.

Later on, a pod of whales appears. They stay with me for a little while and then hurry purposely down the strait. While they are abreast of *Morag Anne* they stand on their tails and slap back on the water in a great display. I haven't the slightest concern about the whales. They have never bothered me. It was interesting to read an account of Shackleton's magnificent voyage from Elephant Island to South Georgia, and to discover that he and his crew were concerned when killer whales appeared.

Shackleton's boat, the one he and his men took to after *Discovery* was held in Antarctic ice, was called the *James Caird* and can be seen in the National Maritime Museum at Greenwich. I say it can be seen but I must tell you that it is not on prominent display — not as prominently as I think it deserves to be. When I went there to see it, some years ago, I had to work hard.

"Here," shouted one uniformed attendant to another, "this cove wants to see the *James Caird.*"

"Oh no," was the reply, "not the *James Caird!* It's in the basement somewhere. Gorblimey, what a caper!"

And grumbling all the way, he led me outside, down a flight of steps and through various rooms like dungeons before showing me the very boat that Shackleton and his men dragged across the ice and sailed by dead reckoning for hundreds of miles, a feat of navigation to rival that of Captain William Bligh. Shackleton was a great man, eclipsing that other explorer of Antarctica, Robert Falcon Scott, who was undoubtedly brave but foolhardy.

Shackleton, who was certainly just as brave, was a planner, cautious and sensible and, what's more, he brought his crew home. He is one of my heroes.

I spend the night in Knox Bay, Thurlow Island. Captain Vancouver did the same thing on July 12, 1792. However, since he was one day out in his reckoning, having forgotten to take the International Date Line into account as he crossed the Pacific, perhaps it was the13th. I like to think it was because that's my birthday.

The tide turns before I get as far as the bay. I have to hug the shore and make use of every back eddy which is always exciting and gives me the pleasant sense of getting something for nothing inasmuch as I shouldn't be making any headway at all against the tide.

By this time I am getting rather fed up with Johnstone Strait and the vagaries of its currents, tides and bores. When Mayne Passage opens on the port side I don't hesitate to turn away from the strait. I will pass through the Yuculta Rapids rather than Surge Narrows and the prospect doesn't bother me. Surge Narrows and I have seen enough of each other.

I come upon Blind Channel where there is a magnificent hotel and a good general store. The young lady in the store is so tickled when she learns how I am travelling that she gives me a free banana and it's not every day something like that happens. There are all sorts of advantages to having a pretty little boat.

At Blind Channel marina I moor right behind the largest private cruising vessel I have ever seen. She is registered to Juneau, Alaska. Her size and gilt gingerbread appearance notwithstanding, a brown and wrinkled elderly gentleman whom I take to be the owner, leans over the rail and tells me what a fine-looking boat I have. Under the circumstances, I think this is mighty nice of him. The contrast between our boats could hardly be greater. He is disposed to chat and even whistles up his skipper and gets him to consult his charts, and for some unknown reason, his computer to find out what sort of conditions I can expect further up the channel. The verdict is that I shall have no trouble. I must say I haven't been worrying very much but it is good of him to bother and I set off reassured, which is always a comfortable feeling to have in a small open boat.

Blind Channel is one of the many places I would like to revisit. A couple of days spent in comfort and luxury in such a beautiful spot would be great. Of course to satisfy my Presbyterian conscience, I would have to work to get there so it would mean going in *Morag Anne* or something similar. Hedonism is only permissible up to a point. After that it becomes downright wicked and we know what lies in store for the wicked.

By this stage of the voyage, without a great deal of sailing time, I am well settled into the routine of rowing all day or most of it. My hands are comfortably calloused and the old muscles don't creak too much. It is a grand life, and as a bonus, the sun shines every day.

On the way to Yuculta, Mayne Passage meets Cordero Channel. The meeting of the waters is turbulent enough to be a bother. Broken, confused sea, whirlpools and overfalls and all kinds of debris from wood chips to big trees with their roots attached, swirling and bobbing all around. The whirlpools are not in the Surge Narrows class but they can't be ignored. To make things more interesting and adding a little unusual excitement, the channel is filled with boats of all shapes and sizes. They are hurrying to beat the change of the tide.

I mean to spend the night at Shoal Bay and to pass through the Yuculta proper next day. If I can't manage to do this in one tide, then I plan to find somewhere safe to tie up for the second night. Finding somewhere safe might not be so simple for the tidal current may reach ten knots or more. I am turning this over in my mind, and at the same time, watching the approach of a very dark and ominous looking cloud when a yacht under power comes close from behind.

"Could you use a tow?"

The vernacular reply is "Could I ever!" and in short order I am sitting in the cockpit of *Mandala,* coffee mug in my hand and watching *Morag Anne* bobbing merrily in the yacht's wake. The expression *deus ex machina* would not be inappropriate. Or perhaps, "You lucky dog, Leighton, fallen on your feet again."

Mandala is also making for Shoal Bay. I anchor beside her, and wonder of wonders, manage to get up the tent before the rain starts in earnest. Even better than that, I am invited for a great dinner by Robert Charleson and his crew. It is a magnificent paella which Robert, a gourmet cook, prepares with elaborate care. When he ferries me back to *Morag Anne* it is all I can do to drag my distended stomach over the transom. I collapse into my sleeping bag, beatifically full.

In addition to filling me with paella, Robert and his merry men convince me that I should take a tow through Yuculta next day. He has sailed these waters for years and he is quite adamant that I will be running a needless risk to try to get through under oar power.

In the event, it is impressive to observe how meticulously Robert brings us through with strict timing such that we pass each danger spot in the mile or two of the rapids at precisely the right time which is, of course, slack water. This is something that I would never have been able to achieve.

I am not suggesting that it can't be done and in fact I'm sure someone or maybe even many people have brought small boats through Yuculta without a motor. I'll simply say that, for my part, I was very glad to have Robert's and *Mandala's* help. Added to that, of course, is the bonus of great company. I am sad to part with such pleasant people at Big Bay on Stuart Island.

The sea is calm, the day is fine and I have a slight current to carry me down the channel. I pass the famous Blow Hole and the Rendezvous Islands and find a tiny exposed bay on Cortes, in Lewis Channel in the late afternoon. The wind is whistling up the channel, pushing a steep sea before it. It is hopeless to think of battling the two together. I throw the anchor into a forest of kelp and settle for the night without bothering to put up the tent.

I sleep for an hour or two. When I wake, it is a fine night. The stars are bright and there is not a breath of wind. The sea is a dead flat calm. I would be better off to turn over and sleep the rest of the night in my little kelp-ridden cove. But the siren call to get on is too strong. Squirrel Cove is a mere eight miles down the channel.

After a herculean struggle with the anchor and the kelp I start to row down the channel by starlight and everything goes well for about an hour and a half. Then, little by little, everything goes wrong. The night clouds over, the wind begins to blow, the sea becomes rough and rougher yet.

Rain starts, then falls in a cold deluge. I creep along a rocky shore, from headland to headland, standing and straining at the oars and making painfully slow progress.

This is undoubtedly the worst and hardest thing I have experienced in the whole adventure. I keep looking over my shoulder for any sign of the flashing light that will show the entrance to Squirrel Cove. A couple of hours go by and still no light. I admit I am getting desperate.

Finally, and none too soon, comes the light and the point. I just get around it, my starboard oar scraping the barnacles of the rock.

Half a mile away is a bright light which I take to be on the government wharf. I row towards it in calm water. Almost miraculously the rain stops, clouds part and the stars are bright again. I can't think who will be out and about at such an hour in Squirrel Cove but, thank goodness, there is someone. I never see his face but he calls out as I approach the wharf,

"A fine night for a row."

He takes my line, ties it to a stanchion and disappears into the night. Somehow I get up the tent, dry the floor, unroll my sleeping bag and collapse into an exhausted sleep.

A little stiff and remarkably hungry, I wake eight hours later and decide that a day's rest in Squirrel Cove would do me no harm. I am watching my billy boil and rubbing sleep from my eyes when a cheerful hail announces the arrival of *Mandala* to refuel. Robert doesn't linger but it is a pleasant reunion and I wave them away from the wharf with a deep sense of regret mixed with gratitude for their kindness and hospitality.

During the course of an exploratory walk through the village of Squirrel Cove I come across three men contemplating a pile of lumber in the gently falling rain.

"Good day, sirs. Is there, by any chance, somewhere a man can get a shower around here?"

"Funny you should ask," says the obvious spokesman for the group, a grizzled Indian gentleman. "We're just on the point of starting to build one."

"Yes," says a second, "come back next year."

All hands thereupon collapse in mirth.

So, no shower but a good rest and I am away on the dawn tide in the morning. In Malaspina Strait, not a mile from Bliss Harbour which sounds a great place although I never see it, I am overtaken by a flotilla of seine boats roaring down the strait. The leading boat veers towards me and slows.

"Getting your morning exercise, eh?"

I am happy to rest for a moment and explain the situation to a friendly skipper whose name is Jack Darlen and who, when he hears my story, invites me to come aboard, have some coffee and take a tow down to Vancouver if I want.

I say the coffee would be more than welcome and a tow to Savary Island would be just fine.

Jack is soon on his radio to the skippers of the other boats.

"Fellows, you'll never guess what I have here. It's an old coot who says he's rowing back to Vancouver and he's been up to Blunden."

"Jack," comes a reply from the ether, "he's havin' you on."

Jack seems satisfied with my credentials. We have a pleasant trip to Savary and part bosom friends which is the way of things in these encounters.

If it hasn't done so already this is starting to sound like a chapter of accidents but I must, I suppose, be truthful. Otherwise this will be a novel and not the account of a real voyage. The truth is, I would have done well to capitalize on my good luck and spend the night at Savary or, at the very least, at Harwood which is within sight of the tall chimney stacks of the Powell River mill and would have made an admirable jumping-off place for the next day.

Instead, those very chimneys drag me onwards, ever onwards and by the time I am a mile or two from them and close to the shore, I am once again in deep trouble for the tide has turned ferociously against me. I am making no headway. A sensible man would cut his losses and retreat to Harwood. Alas, I am still gripped by the urge to get ahead at all costs.

Powell River is now tantalisingly close, near enough to let me see late afternoon walkers leading their dogs along the shore path. But rocks are all around, and more of them are showing almost by the minute. It doesn't seem at all a friendly place to spend the night.

I could still let the tide carry me back to Harwood. Indeed, in retrospect, there is no question that would have been the sensible thing to do. But, retreat? Perish the thought! If a boy in a small dinghy with a tiny outboard motor hadn't zipped across my bow at this moment I would have had to accept fate anyway, hearts of oak and boys of the bulldog breed and what not put to one side. As it is, I persuade him to tow me towards the mill and, when he runs out of gasoline and casts me loose in the still rapid tide, kind fortune casts me against a father and son who, fishing over for the day, are making for their berth in nearby Westview. They kindly tow me there. *Deus ex machina* again.

I spend the night in a hotel but I can't say that I sleep there. The first hotel is advertising live music in the bar until two a.m. and the woman in reception advises going somewhere else. She is good enough to call a taxi which takes me to a second hotel. The fly in the ointment is the fact that a wedding reception is in progress and it too goes on into the small hours. It is a very warm night. The wedding party leaves windows and French doors open and strolls about, cooling off, wine glasses in their hands, close beneath the window of my room. I can't grudge them their fun and pleasure but it is a sleepless night and I leave the hotel very early in the morning. To get a bit of exercise, stretch my legs and clear my head, I run down to the marina where the boat is moored. It is a shock to find the gate locked.

By the greatest stroke of luck, the only man I know in Powell River decides to go fishing this morning. Less than a minute after I arrive at the locked gate he is at my side, unlocking it.

It is a pleasant row down Malaspina Strait to Scotch Fir Point where I anchor for a late lunch. There are no Scotch firs that I can see, but there is a lovely old farm, pasture and fruit trees, an idyllic place. I am afraid I enjoy it too much and stay too long.

When I come to leave I find the wind has got up and there is a nasty choppy sea where Jervis Inlet joins the strait. This makes for difficult rowing and, with yesterday's experience in mind, I am actually thinking of retreat when I come across *Puffin,* a converted seine boat. I am invited on board, and before they give me a big piece of coffee cake, I am shown the rock cod they have just caught. I suppose I should be ashamed to admit this is the first rock cod I have seen. I had no idea they were so big. Before I set off on this adventure several people advised me to take rod and line and live off the sea. I am glad I didn't. If I ever caught a fish this size I don't know what I would have done. I might have boiled a tiny fraction in my billy perhaps but I would have had to throw the rest over the side.

Puffin is the most completely renovated fishing boat I have ever seen. The main cabin has a carpet, a corner fireplace complete with a surround of Dutch tiles, sofa, chairs and an oak table with a floral arrangement in a magnificent Japanese vase. O'Sullivan's dictum, "any fool can be uncomfortable" and its inescapable corollary that it's a wise man who isn't, spring again to mind.

Next morning I have the deuce of a time getting around Cockburn Point. *Deuce,* from the Latin *duo* or two, the lowest throw of the dice. What interesting things words are. One die, two dice; derived from *dare,* to give or cast, also Latin of course. I'm not certain how or why it became a synonym for the devil. Perhaps it was an expression of disgust when the player found he had got such a poor throw. Who cares, many would ask.

Any way, devil, deuce or whatever, Cockburn is a challenge in the teeth of a gale. I barely scrape around under the light at the point, but when I immediately hoist my sail I am blown down the strait, clean past Pender Harbour, Francis Island and as far as Macnaughten Point and Smuggler Cove before the wind dies to nothing and the sun shines from a cloudless sky. Had it not been for that grand sail my spirits might have wilted before Roberts Creek.

I suppose I should be a bit downcast; after all when I was last here on my first night at sea, I had high expectations, hopes of reaching Prince Rupert. In point of fact, I couldn't be more happy for it has all been a priceless adventure. Lucky Leighton indeed. Cape Caution and Rupert can wait.

Next morning it is a breathlessly calm day. I intend to head towards Point Roberts and to cross the strait to Galiano and leave the boat in Whaler Bay. Greg Foster will take care of her.

It is a long, hot row that seems to last forever. Ponderous freighters lie anchored, high-hulled or deep-laden, waiting for a berth at the overcrowded docks inside the harbour. Power boats skitter about. Civilization. For a moment I am tempted to turn around. What a letdown. Garbage and weed slosh in an oily swell.

It is a relief to get behind the breakwater at Point Grey where the sounds are cheerful. The beach is crowded with people, most of them stark naked and healthily pink in the setting sun.

It is a very different scene the following morning. Clouds are down almost to the waterline along the North Shore, a choppy sea around the breakwater. There is a scent of rain in the air. No matter, I think, I'll give it a go. I row out of the booming grounds, around the light at the end of the breakwater and look down the gulf. It is not a cheerful sight; clouds are scudding up the strait, the sea is lumpy and unpleasant. A flotilla of gill-netters makes its way toward Burrard Inlet. As *Morag Anne* lies rolling and tossing while I assess the situation, one of them changes course and approaches. A bearded face calls out, "Trouble?"

"Not really, trying to decide what to do. I want to get down to Point Roberts."

"Got a motor?"

"No."

"Well, wouldn't really matter if you had, you won't get far in that little boat anyway. It's as rough out there as I've ever seen it. Too rough for me and all those others," pointing to the gill-netters. "You'd better stay where you are. You're not in trouble now, but boy oh boy, you sure as heck will be if you go out there."

Sometimes it's nice to have your mind made up for you.

Jericho it will be. Dry land moorage. Nothing wrong with that.

It is a pleasant, early morning row past all the harbour marks. Wreck Beach, guard towers, sand-bank warnings, concession buildings and finally, Jericho Beach.

As the keel slides up the sand, a man briskly walking his dog looks over and calls, "Nice day for a row."

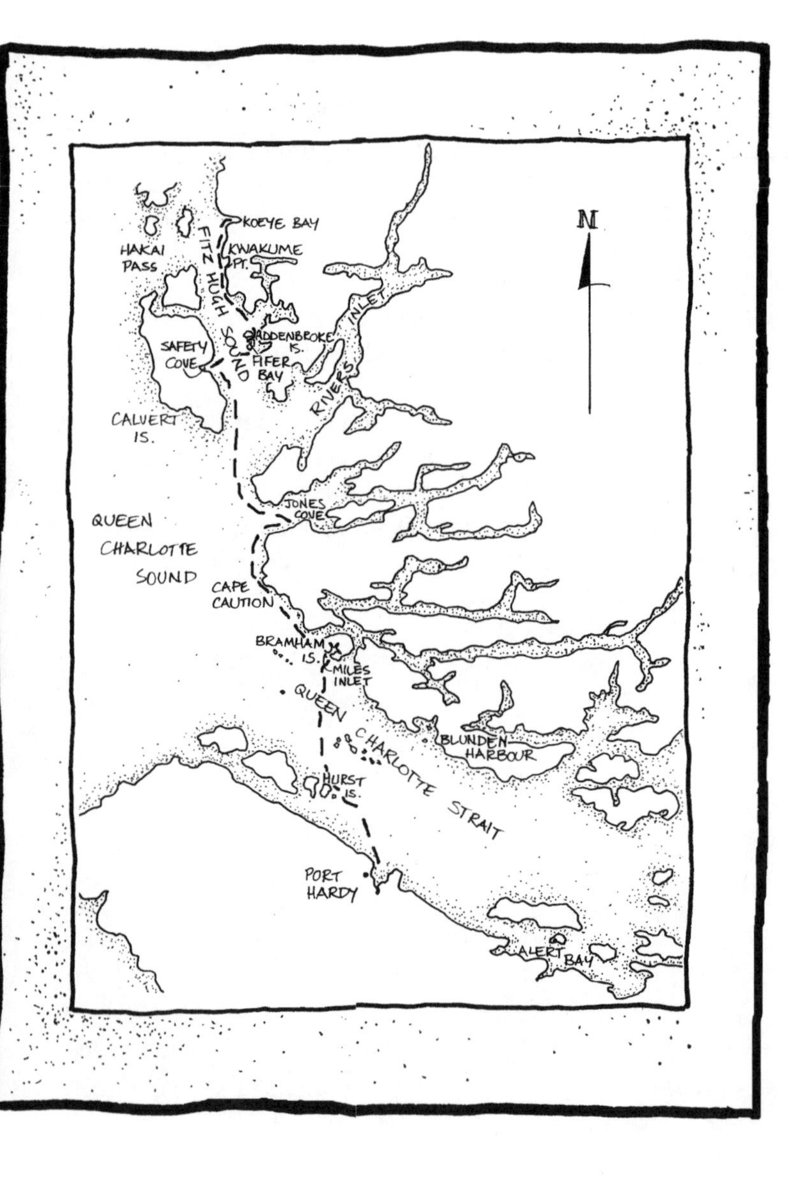
N
KOEYE BAY
KWAKUME PT.
HAKAI PASS
FITZ HUGH SOUND
ADDENBROKE IS.
SAFETY COVE
FIFER BAY
RIVERS INLET
CALVERT IS.
JONES COVE
QUEEN CHARLOTTE SOUND
CAPE CAUTION
BRAMHAM IS.
MILES INLET
QUEEN CHARLOTTE STRAIT
BLUNDEN HARBOUR
HURST IS.
PORT HARDY
ALERT BAY

Chapter Eight

Once more unto the breach, dear friends,
once more.
Shakespeare, HENRY V

IT IS JUNE 1993. *Morag Anne* has not yet reached Prince Rupert. Nineteen ninety-two had its own adventures but the jollyboat was not part of them. It is time to complete the voyage and realise the dream. It is a long way from Vancouver to Blunden Harbour and because I have covered the distance twice, there and back, I have decided to launch the boat at Port Hardy.

True to form, the launching is not an auspicious occasion. There is trouble right away. Getting the trailer and boat into the water is easy for the ramp slopes steeply down. Hanging onto the boat's painter, however, I am startled to see the trailer shoot off on its own and disappear into the oily, dirty water of the harbour. The tide is rising.

The sensible thing to do is to wait for the ebb but I am impatient to be off. I hope I learn a lesson from what follows.

The sun is still high and reflected light makes it difficult to see beneath the surface of the water. We cruise around with Nancy hanging over the bow calling directions. This sort of thing can strain the tightest of matrimonial bonds and it is fortunate that we discover the trailer before too long. It is under the wharf, caught in the pilings.

There is no one in sight as I strip to my underwear. However, by the time I am standing on the wharf, eyeing the unattractive water, quite a crowd has gathered.

One of the bystanders calls out, "Take my pike pole to shove the line under the trailer."

This is excellent advice as I find out when I finally accept it. First, as usual, I have to try doing things my way. To everyone's obvious amusement I lower myself into the water and try to dive to the trailer which is deeper than it seems. I can't pass the wretched rope around anything on the trailer and eventually I do what I should have done — I use the proffered pike pole and have no difficulty in passing the rope around something invisible on the rear of the trailer. My new fisherman friend takes the rope and hitches it to his truck. When he starts off, a bar with the trailer's rear lights and a gaggle of wires rises from the water at the end of the rope.

At this point I sensibly leave the salvage operations in the capable hands of my helpful fisherman and in hardly any time he has the trailer on dry land. I decide to cut my losses and delay departure until the morrow.

Jerry Arnet, my fisherman, tells me to raft my boat alongside his beautiful old seiner, the *Blue Sea*. I leave her there, confident that she will be safe with Jerry.

We spend the night in a hot, noisy motel where sleep is a lost cause. The ignominy of the trailer fiasco is uppermost in my mind and I replay the scene about a hundred times. Leighton, I say again and again, will you never learn? I can imagine the comments of the Great Hugh Macartney, my guide, philosopher, friend and mentor. The trouble is, they would all be well deserved. Oh, dear.

Next day is anticlimactic. Nothing goes wrong. We load the last of the supplies. Jerry Arnet gives me his advice about courses, tides and Cape Caution and tells me the latest weather report. Nancy, car and trailer leave for Vancouver and I set off for Prince Rupert. Prince Rupert? Well, anyway, I set off.

Hardy Bay is long and wide. Not another boat is in sight. Some islands look blue on the horizon but the farther shore of the strait is invisible. Rupert might be the goal. But first, Cape Caution!

Nancy's last words to me were, "Remember, you're to enjoy this. Don't feel you must go hurrying on, you've got no deadline. Make the most of it. But, above all, enjoy it." Good advice.

Mountain Equipment Co-op in Vancouver sells ski gloves with padded leather palms. I bought a pair although experience makes me skeptical. Blisters have always been my lot at the start of any rowing expedition in the past. For once, my skepticism is unfounded. The gloves perform admirably. I recommend them to any rower. An extra thick foam rubber cushion proves a godsend. A bag of hard candies on the thwart beside me and the world is as right as rain. The sun shines. Everything is going so well it is uncanny.

I spend a comfortable night in Harlequin Bay on Hurst Island, determinedly not giving a thought to Cape Caution and beyond.

By next evening I am at Miles Inlet, Bramham Island, on the north side of the strait. It has been a foggy, drizzly day. Walkers and Deserters Islands are only shadows in the mist as I row slowly across, keeping a steady two knots for seven hours.

I could allow myself to worry — this is the jumping-off point for the attempt to round the cape. My weather radio cannot pick up Alert Bay clearly. It is aggravating to hear "This is Alert Bay Coast Guard Radio" without difficulty and then a burst of static with here and there words like "... from the west" and "... fifteen rising to twenty-five knots." I am about to settle down for the night, not quite certain what my plan of action should be when a lovely little Folkboat, the *Eight by Ten* comes nosing up the inlet. I wave and ask if they can get the forecast.

"Early morning calm with wind rising to twenty-five knots from the northwest by noon."

That is it, then. The way to go is clear. Set off late tonight, get around the cape at or soon after dawn, if this is possible, and slip into the first crack in the coast I come across. Everything will hinge on the breaking swell at the cape. Am I apprehensive? Well, of course I am. Failing to get around the cape for the second time would be too much altogether, but on the other hand, I can't control the elements.

Anyone who has bought one of those modern watches with an alarm and all the other gadgets knows that adjusting them is exasperating. After a great deal of experimentation and still not quite sure it will rouse me at midnight,

I settle down to a few hours of anxious rest. I can't call it sleep.

I leave the inlet in a cloud of mosquitoes. There is a faint moon, hidden intermittently by heavy banks of cloud. Deadheads and debris near the shoreline are a nuisance but not a real hazard. All the same, it's disconcerting to hit something with a solid thud in the dark.

I row hard, very hard. Then I remember Nancy's parting advice and change from frantic effort to a slow, steady pull.

The lighthouse at Cape Caution is automated, but thank goodness, it blinks steadily. I keep its beam off my starboard bow for the rest of what is left of the night when I am well and truly out in the strait which takes longer than I expect. But I am making progress in the right direction. It is exciting to be so close to Cape Caution at last.

I keep far from the shore, rising high on the swell that comes broadside towards the boat. There are no breaking waves this far out and the motion of the swell, a big swell to be sure, is just pleasantly exhilarating.

It seems to take forever to get round the cape. Dawn comes and I can see the lighthouse. But by this time at least, it is abeam. This means I am there, actually and truly abreast of Cape Caution. I know I am going to make it this time. Just keep on rowing, steady and hard and I will get it behind me, once and for all. It is a tremendous feeling that makes me long for my companion. Sharing these moments of triumph is more satisfying than their solitary enjoyment. When you have been married as long as I have, such moments cry out for sharing.

Dawn comes slowly with blood-red clouds low on the horizon. My bare knees are cold. A small wind blows from the west. Soon it is bright day and a full gale. I use the term loosely, of course. I have no way to judge the force of the wind but it feels like a gale and I am very pleased to find Jones Cove, an hour after passing the cape. The entrance is a narrow crack and the cove is well protected from almost any wind. I have the place to myself for a couple of hours while I lie at anchor in the sunshine and savour the pleasure of finally conquering Cape Caution.

I'm not a bit disturbed when a large motor cruiser arrives, followed soon after by my friends of the night before, Walter and Maxine Goad of the *Eight by Ten*. Of course, I don't know their names yet, that comes later. They look quite wet and weather beaten.

"We had a brisk time getting here," they say. "It was blowing hard, the sea was almost more than we could handle. More than we bargained for."

After a while the cruiser's skipper comes in his inflatable dinghy. After the usual remarks about my pretty little boat he invites me for dinner. Not the least concerned that I had just had cream of wheat and noodles, I accept at once.

That is when I discover the names of my various companions and yet another example of the remarkable coincidences that life affords. The cruiser is named *Lycon*. Her owner is Ian Falconer who spent part of his boyhood on the island of North Uist, which is in the Outer Hebrides of Scotland and where I practised medicine before coming to Canada. He has, as we say, some Gaelic. His aunt and uncle had been my patients. I don't run into an *Uisteach* very often and most people would have a hard time finding the island on a map. This meeting and at this time, Cape Caution and all, is almost too much to credit. We have a great *ceilidh*.

The next morning is grey and misty. As I row past *Lycon* on my way out of the bay, Ian calls out to me, "The forecast is terrible. Let me give you a tow over to Calvert Island; that'll get you into shelter for the rest of the day."

Looking at the cold, lumpy sea outside Jones Cove it is hard to refuse. The prospect of breakfast with Ian and Vivienne makes the decision that much easier.

Lycon is bound for Bella Coola. When Ian says goodbye a mile or two from the shore of Calvert Island, I am in cold Fitz Hugh Sound, on a choppy sea with misty mountains on both sides of the channel and very pleased not to be in the open sea of Queen Charlotte Sound.

I row into Safety Cove on Calvert. It is a wide bay rather than a cove and I don't think it would be all that safe in most weathers. I find it a gloomy place but eat a second breakfast. When I come to leave I find that the wind changed while I ate and has blown away the clouds. It is ready to blow me up the sound at such pace I don't even bother to put the sail up.

It is a good, sunny, fresh and breezy day and I leave any cares and worries in Safety Cove and let the anchor down in Fifer Bay, Blair Island, as the sun sets behind Calvert Island on the other side of the sound.

I am warm and comfortable, sheltered from the wind by a forest of pine and arbutus, the last arbutus I am to see on this voyage. The scent is both languorous and sensuous.

Someone is clearing land on top of the bluff across the bay using a seine boat, a line to the trees and a lot of bad language. There are few things more enjoyable than watching someone hard at work on a late afternoon in summer. I have a ringside seat.

I have a lot of hard work to do myself next day and most of it is my own fault. I set off when the ebb is on the turn and hope that the flood won't be fierce. Anyway, it is a fine morning and I am full of beans.

The lighthouse and the keepers' houses on Addenbrooke pass in pretty good style and bright sunshine. They look delightfully idyllic although I think there was some nasty story about a murder there many years ago. Today, the whole place has such a pleasant, peaceful air that I decide I wouldn't mind a job there and wonder for a while how a man would set about applying for it.

Things get a little sticky after this. The sun disappears and clouds come down. Everything is damp and humid for there is no breeze at all. The tide turns against me, more strongly than I like, and rowing is slow and hard. I am starting to feel sorry for myself when, at Kwakume Point, two things happen to cheer me up. First there is a school of dolphins, at least fifty of them. They come close to the boat cavorting and rolling in synchrony. It is an amazing sight and it sounds like a waterfall or a river in spate.

The second thing that happens is the appearance of *Eight by Ten* with Walter and Maxine Goad. We exchange greetings, Walter in a yellow sou'wester and Maxine popping her head up from the cabin to wish me well. These brief, chance meetings at sea are heartening reminders that perhaps the human race is not such a mistake after all. The Goads and their boat soon disappear in the mist and I row until a breeze gets up from the north to blow it away. Not long after the day becomes clear, I meet a Dutch cruise ship going north and then the *Royal Viking,* a white, silent ghost very much closer than the Dutchman. Love Boats aplenty. Fitz Hugh Sound is wide enough for us all and I am close to the eastern shore but I like it best when I can see these big ships from afar. It is frightening when they come out of a fog. If I were directly in their path I couldn't get out of the way.

Soon, the *Spirit of the North,* the B.C. government ferry, passes on her way from Port Hardy to Prince Rupert. She alters course and slows down for a minute or two. Passengers line the rails and wave. I wave back. She is an elegant ship, a cut above the barge-like ferries running between the mainland and Vancouver Island.

As I approach Koeye Bay, searching the coastline for the cabin that the *Coastal Pilot* says marks the entrance, a big metal seine boat comes alongside, the *Windward Island* of Nanaimo. An oriental head with many gold teeth sticks out of the wheelhouse.

"Are you in trouble?"

I say I am okay and make to get on with my rowing for the tide is carrying us both back down the sound. However, he is inclined to talk.

"Is this some kind of world expedition?"

No it isn't but how can I describe what I am about? I say yes, it is something like that. Two crewmen in spotless white singlets smile as the powerful diesels engage. The stern dips, the metal monster surges ahead.

Koeye is a pleasant bay with a curving silver beach. A river curls down from the left as you approach. I anchor inside a rocky spit guarding the entrance.

It is fairly calm inside the bay but the wind howls all night in the trees and surf crashes against the rocky entrance. Spray comes over the spit and patters on my tent. I can't pretend I sleep well.

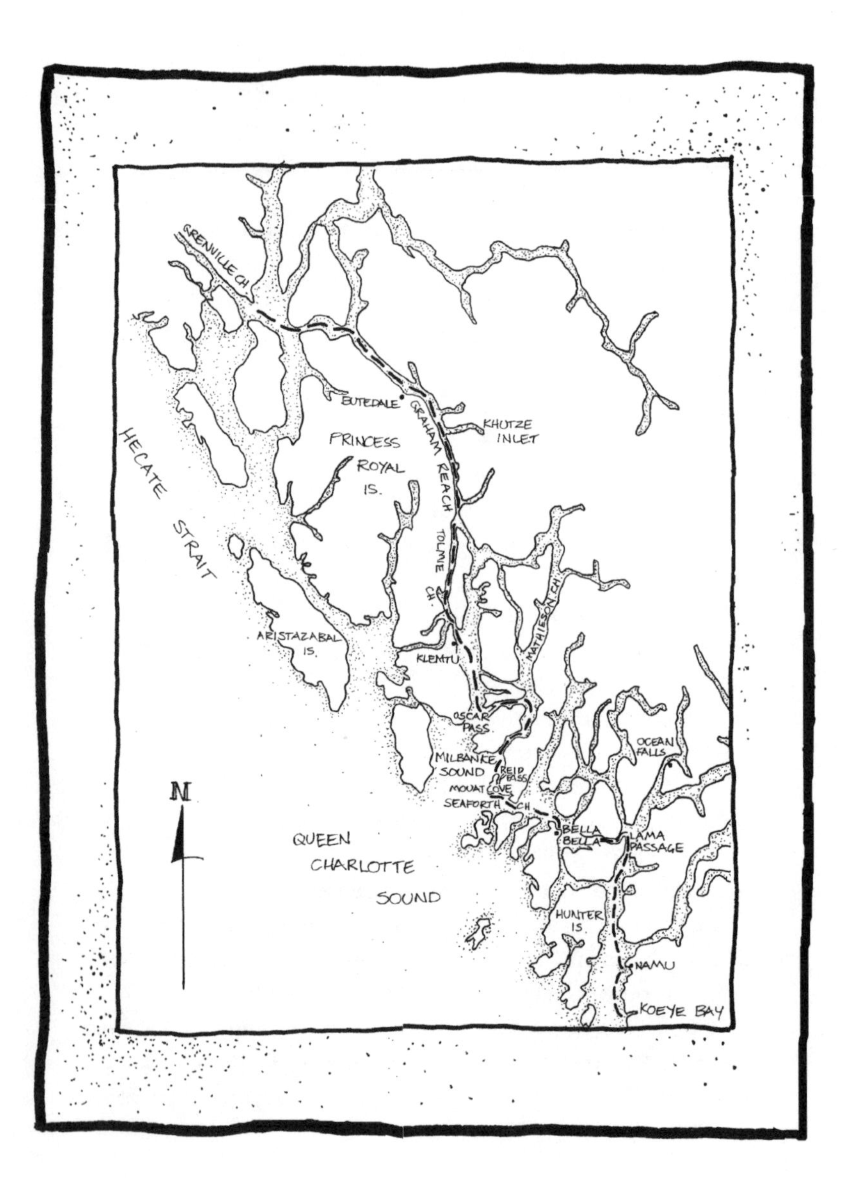
GRENVILLE CH
BUTEDALE
GRAHAM REACH
KHUTZE INLET
PRINCESS ROYAL IS.
HECATE STRAIT
TOLMIE CH.
MATHIESON CH
ARISTAZABAL IS.
KLEMTU
OSCAR PASS.
OCEAN FALLS
MILBANKE SOUND
REID PASS
MOUAT COVE
SEAFORTH CH
BELLA BELLA
LAMA PASSAGE
QUEEN CHARLOTTE SOUND
HUNTER IS.
NAMU
KOEYE BAY
N

Chapter Nine

But the peaceful Summer cruises or quiet week-ends which constitute the greater proportion of one's sailing experiences, are apt to make dull reading ....

Eric Hiscock, COME ABOARD

IT IS A grey morning and surf is breaking around the entrance to Koeye, but thank goodness, once outside the cove there is nothing more alarming than a heavy swell and very little wind to bother me as I row up the channel to Namu. For some reason or other I am keen to see Namu, maybe because of all I have read about the early days of the fishing. A great fleet of small long-liners brought their catches to the cannery. In any case, there will be a telephone, a general store and a wharf where I can moor and go ashore to stretch my legs. All in all, Namu is today's lodestone.

It is a long, steady row for most of the day. Several gill-netters roar past. I can clearly see the faces of the men at the wheel but for all the attention they pay to *Morag Anne* and me we might be invisible. By late afternoon I am making my way through small island channels past deserted boardwalks and weathered clapboard sheds. Eventually the bay opens out. I can see no sign of a government wharf. In fact, the one sign of life, if that's what you could call it, is a solitary individual leaning against the wheelhouse of his gill-netter which is moored with several others at a very private looking wharf. I take a chance and row across.

"I can't seem to find the government wharf."

"There isn't one, that's why. There isn't anything. The place is shut, closed down. Nothing here at all."

What a letdown. No store, no telephone, no one to talk to apart from this man who doesn't appear very friendly. He hasn't shifted his position by an inch, can of beer in hand and cigarette stuck like glue to his lower lip. I don't fancy going for much of a walk either, for the whole place has a gloomy, depressed air about it.

Well, you can't win 'em all.

Two more, equally depressed-looking men show up. One says, "I seen you out there on the sound. I says to myself, 'Who's that crazy old coot out there rowing his boat?'"

"Well, now you know."

"Yeah, and just as crazy as he looked, I guess."

This conversation is clearly going nowhere but I tie up and go ashore anyway. It is a ghost town. Everything is shut. The inhabitants appear to have left in something of a hurry and not very long ago. A thin, lonely dog barks from around the corner of a warehouse. Garbage bags rustle in the wind. I am happy to get back on *Morag Anne* and push off. The morose fishermen watch me leave. No one speaks. They may have been pleased to see me go. If that is the case, they are no more pleased than I am to be leaving the gloomy place.

Before I can get the anchor down and the tent up in the next little cove I come to, the heavens open and the boat and I are soaked. It seems a fitting end to a poor day. Things can't get any worse, so I cheer up immensely and open a tin of sardines.

Namu is notorious for whirlwinds. I don't encounter any which is something to be grateful for. It is said they have laid large boats on their sides. I anchor close to the shore for the protection of the tall trees at the water's edge. Prepared for the worst, nothing happens. The best way to keep the rain at bay is to take an umbrella.

The weather up to this point has been good apart from the inevitable showers that are a fixture of summer conditions on the coast. They wet you and are a nuisance if the boat is wet when you put up the tent, but they don't lower the spirits. If they do, you shouldn't be in a small open boat. However, on the way to Bella Bella from Namu the weather turns decidedly nasty. It rains steadily and the wind blows a gale from the southeast. I hear later that it caused havoc and destruction up and down the coast. That is unfortunate, of course, but the same wind blows me to Bella Bella in jig time.

I go through Lama Passage faster than I have any right to, literally pushed by both tide and gale. It is exciting and the landmarks come and go with astonishing speed. I can't take time to look at the chart but there is only one way to go. I am well protected inside oilskins. A sou'wester sheds the water satisfactorily without dripping it down the back of my neck. This is the great advantage the sou'wester has over all other rain hats.

Waves surge past, lifting the boat and hurrying her onwards. Spume flies from the breakers. Goodness knows how fast I am going but the shore speeds by in a blur of cloud, rain and spray. The one danger is that of broaching in the trough of a wave and getting swamped by the curling comber that follows. I row as hard as possible so as to keep way on in the hollows. It is tremendously exhilarating.

I approach the village of Bella Bella which is visible from far off, white houses against a dark forest background. In an aluminum dinghy two Indian boys are trolling, their parka hoods over their heads, faces expressionless as they pass not ten feet from *Morag Anne.* I am a bit euphoric. First of all, I have made an amazingly fast passage from the time the wind started, faster than ever before. Then there is the thrill of getting to Bella Bella.

"Hi there!"

I could have saved my breath for there is no response. I am another intruder, crazy enough to be rowing from goodness knows where. It is a miserable day anyway.

I find the government wharf and fill a water container. The supermarket is run by the Indian band and is pleasantly relaxed. There is no muzak, thank goodness. I can't think what I need. The shelves are bursting with the usual things you find in supermarkets. Fishermen are stocking up with vast amounts of meat, fruit and baked goods. I buy some postcards to send to various friends telling them that I have reached Bella Bella. I guess I am pretty pleased with myself for having got so far in so short a time.

This is a bank card age. Before I left Vancouver I made certain that my bank had a branch in Bella Bella. What I didn't discover was that it is open an hour or two once or twice a week. This is not one of those times, so I go to the hospital where I explain my predicament to the administrator, and she most obligingly cashes my personal cheque. I don't think I would find a hospital administrator who would do the same for me in Vancouver. God bless people in small towns.

It is good to be able to stretch my legs but Bella Bella doesn't really encourage a long visit. Indian fishermen leaning against the railings of the government wharf are friendly but not much use in the matter of advice for rowing boats. The gas boat has been around for too many generations. Three of them separately tell me the drinking water in Bella Bella is no good and better water can be found at Klemtu. They talk as if Klemtu is just around the corner. Bella Bella water looks good enough to me so I leave my newly acquired stock where it is. Goodness only knows when or if I will reach Klemtu.

I seem to have exhausted the attractions of Bella Bella. I start to think about leaving when I see the Coast Guard boat coming into the bay. It is making very heavy weather of the passage from the other side of the channel. I couldn't row against anything like that. There is nothing for it but to find somewhere to anchor and wait for better weather.

The harbour is surprisingly unprotected. Every scrap of wharf or dock space is already occupied by boats escaping the storm. In the end I go to the lee of a small island at the north end of the bay and drop anchor.

The storm rages all night. The anchor drags. About one o'clock in the morning we run onto the rocks. I am up in a flash, pushing the stern away in my pyjamas and rowing for better shelter with the tent still raised. Less than an hour later we blow against a log boom and I spend several hours before dawn clinging to an iron ring and complaining bitterly, which does no good at all.

When dawn eventually comes it is raining hard but I put on foul weather gear and set off for Dryad Point which I pass in a choppy sea with mist swirling around the lighthouse on its lonely rock. In Seaforth Channel as the wind is dropping and the clouds are lifting off the shoreline, *Karen II* from Port Angeles bound for the Alaskan fishery stops to ask if I am okay. I am surprised that the skipper is single-handed but he says he usually fishes alone and with the new arrangement of the drum line forward rather than aft he manages all right. This is the first time I see a drum mounted on the bow; it looks strange but I can see the obvious advantage of watching the line come in.

I am invited on board the *Karen II* but, for once, I decline. This is silly. I am in danger of forgetting Nancy's parting words.

Later, anchored in Mouat Cove, almost knackered after my night of alarms and excursions and very little sleep, I carefully check tide tables and chart. I decide I must be away by eight-thirty in the morning if I am to go through Reid Passage, which is a narrow channel that lets small craft avoid some of the rough waters of Milbanke Sound. I turn in early with this in mind. It is a misty, overcast evening.

I sleep very soundly and wake in bright sunshine. Sleepily I look at my watch. Holy crow! Ten o'clock.

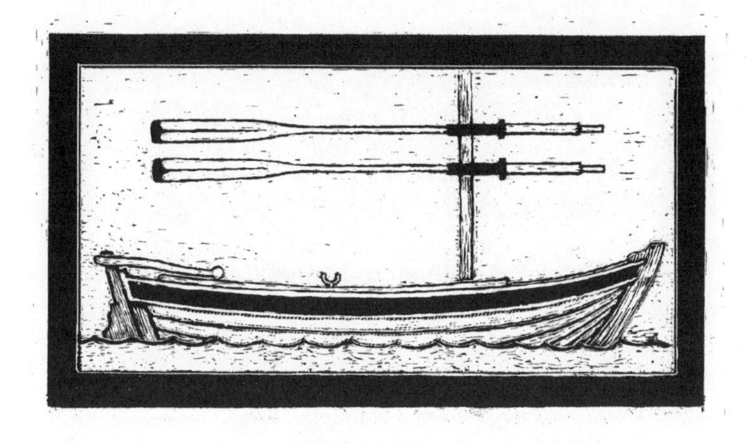

There might still be time to get through Reid Passage if I am lucky. The tent comes down in record time and the anchor is up and stowed in its bucket, and the oars are in the oarlocks in less than fifteen minutes.

I row hard. The sun is hot, beating down from the western sky. The western sky? Hold on, something wrong there. I look at the compass. No doubt about it, the sun is fairly low in the west for all its strength. Then the penny drops. Not ten in the morning, ten at night! Back to the anchorage and up with the tent again.

Everything changes on a fine day. Although the swell coming from Milbanke Sound is Cape Caution over again, with a fine fresh breeze on the port beam, a good breakfast inside me and the tide in my favour, I wish I could cancel the entry in my log for the previous morning which reads,

> *Leaving Bella Bella in violent rain storm. Helly Hansen hood impaired peripheral vision, ran into reef and had to stave off with handle of oar. A fitting departure from rather an unpleasant anchorage. Not even a drink of water inside me. Is this what cruising in open boats is all about? There are times when I think I must be mentally deranged.*

Lots of rocks with surging surf on the approach to Reid Passage keep me farther from shore than usual. The Alaska State Ferry *Columbia* passes close on her way north, decks lined with passengers on my side, most of them waving. The *Columbia* is another real ship, not a floating garage like the ferries on the lower coast which do their jobs well enough but can't be called attractive. The swell is breaking on the rocky shore of Ivory Island with an alarming roar, spray rising at least twenty feet and sweeping inland with the westerly wind. A fearsome place in a storm. Today is nothing.

I have to row around Lizzie Rocks to get into Mathieson Channel. This turns out to be the hardest, toughest row of the voyage. I come within a whisker of turning back. Standing at the oars with one foot forward and pulling with all my might I can just inch forward. Spray flies from the blades at each backward stroke which is itself a stiff push. *Coastal Pilot* instructions are to give the rocks a very wide berth. I try hard to do this but come horribly close to them. They are nasty looking brutes, not sharp like Matterhorns but grey, greasy sullen-looking things like the backs of half-submerged elephants or sinister submarines.

Why is the left side (sinister) considered threatening and bad? I can understand the good things about dexterity. Most people, after all, are right-handed. But the many left-handers are still members of the human race. Leonardo da Vinci was one of them. There is something strange at work here.

I am through Oscar Passage with a following tide before nine o'clock next morning and tie to the dock at Klemtu by four. A long hard row. Cone Island, which looks just that, seemed at first just a hop, skip and a jump away but as the long hot day wore on those hops, skips and jumps seemed to multiply. Around three in the afternoon I remembered that it was Saturday. There is a store in Klemtu where the Coast Guard at Bella Bella had told me I could buy charts that he did not have in stock. Klemtu was at least five miles away when a solitary gill-netter came up from astern. I gave him a wave and he towed me the rest of the way.

I catch the store just before closing time and buy charts, sardines and a few bars of chocolate for I have a sudden craving for something sweet. Is this impulse shopping?

As I come out of the store I hear the most amazing shouting, screaming, clapping and hullabaloo. The Alaska ferry *Columbia* sails ever so slowly past the dock, almost filling the narrow channel. The deck is lined with passengers. Cameras are everywhere. Every inhabitant of Klemtu must be on the boardwalk, waving, shouting, screaming and jumping up and down.

It is all over in a few minutes. The *Columbia* disappears out of sight and the enthusiastic population vanishes. Gulls and crows scavenge the shore and the sun beats down on a silent, empty scene.

I find a pay phone and contact Nancy to reassure her all is well.

Anchored in a little bay behind a log boom, almost in the shadow of an abandoned cannery building from which a boardwalk runs around the bay, I am enjoying the evening sun coming in the open end of the tent when, to my joy and delight, I see the flag of Scotland on *Lycon's* bow coming towards the government wharf. Tent and all I row over to welcome Ian and Vivienne, on their way home from Ocean Falls where the weather has been so good and the houses in the abandoned mill town so inexpensive that Vivienne says they almost bought one on the spot.

It is another evening of good food and talk and at the end of it I am persuaded to spend the night on board in the luxury of a stateroom and luxury it is. It is so comfortable that I sleep badly and waken early to the sound of hundreds of crows. The sun is bright and the air is still. I creep on deck, anxious not to rouse my hosts but with my heart in my mouth for I remember that all my gear is strewn around the boat beneath the tent. Everything, chocolate bars included, is exposed and open to any marauding crow. If I had seen crows actually flying in and out I am not sure what I would have done. Possibly taken my clothes off and swum across. It isn't necessary to do anything so dramatic. The crows ignore *Morag Anne*, intent on easier pickings. I sit on *Lycon's* taffrail and glower at them until Ian calls me for coffee and breakfast.

I say a final farewell and set off up Tolmie Channel.

The sea is calm but not very peaceful. Fish boat after fish boat comes up from astern, heading for the opening of the Nass River season. It may be hard to believe but the wash from these boats is worse than anything from ferries or cruise ships. In addition to that, they go so steadily on, at full speed, that they seem impersonal, blind automata. It is difficult to believe they are under human control. Come to that, if they are on auto-pilot, they aren't. I give them as wide a berth as possible.

I am rowing steadily on a hot, airless morning when along comes *Rosebud,* a beautiful old wooden motor cruiser registered in Jackson Hole, Wyoming, and offers a tow. I am very happy to accept. That is how I meet Jeff Foott, world famous photographer of wildlife, on his way to Alaska. Get out in a small open boat and you meet all sorts of interesting people; it's a fact.

I am towed to Khutze Inlet. The conversation is enjoyable which is why I stay so long with *Rosebud*. You have to take advantage of an encounter like this; a man would be a fool if he didn't.

Jeff is a biologist turned photographer. He has studied seals in Antarctica, climbed in Tibet and guided in the Tetons. He has a wealth of stories and as he is a thoughtful observer I enjoy his company, and he seems pleasantly interested in my saga.

If anything could entice me to go motor cruising, *Rosebud* would be the boat. She is a gem, teak throughout, finished like a Swiss watch, heavy and steady, everything of the highest quality and workmanship.

Next morning I row up Graham Reach and pass the deserted cannery at Butedale in brilliant sunshine. The waterfall is worth a detour. For once I don't have the usual sense of urgency to get on. I think my conversations with Jeff Foott must have had a calming effect, making me realize that there is more to life than just getting to the goal as quickly as possible. Whatever the reason, I happily detour into Butedale and when *Rosebud* overtakes me again and offers another tow, I quickly say yes.

Thus I am at the entrance to Grenville Channel by late afternoon not a bit ashamed at taking such a long tow. It is a day of sun from a cloudless sky and yarn after yarn from Jeff as we sit on his flying bridge and watch Dall dolphins flash white bellies in front of *Rosebud's* bow.

In mid-morning a speck appears on the horizon, growing larger as we draw closer. It alters course towards *Rosebud* and we turn to intercept a kayak which is paddled leisurely by a gnarled, nut-brown veteran smoking a pipe. He cannot be much under sixty-five years of age. His kayak has a red sail brailed around the mast and the old gentleman sits high on an unconventional seat, his feet in large rubber boots. Loose jerrycans possibly containing water lie on the open cockpit floor. He must have other gear but it isn't in evidence. Jeff hails him.

"Where are you coming from and where are you headed?"

"Well now, I set out from Juneau, Alaska and I'm headed for Seattle."

And here am I, thinking I am the adventurous one! It does a man no harm to be taken down a peg or two.

We chat for a while, *Rosebud's* motor idling with the exhaust blowing gentle bubbles at waterline. The kayaker tells us his home is in Florida.

"I've got me an island there. You fellows should come visit me sometime. Don't come in the summer, it's too danged hot. That's why I'm here."

To Jeff he says, "That's a nice little dory you've got there," pointing to *Morag Anne.* I am almost too ashamed to explain I am supposed to be in her and rowing toward Prince Rupert but honesty overcomes embarrassment.

"Is that so? Well lots of luck," and with a laconic wave he dips his paddle in the water and moves off. Jeff and I look at one another. "If I hadn't seen it with my own eyes I wouldn't believe it," he says.

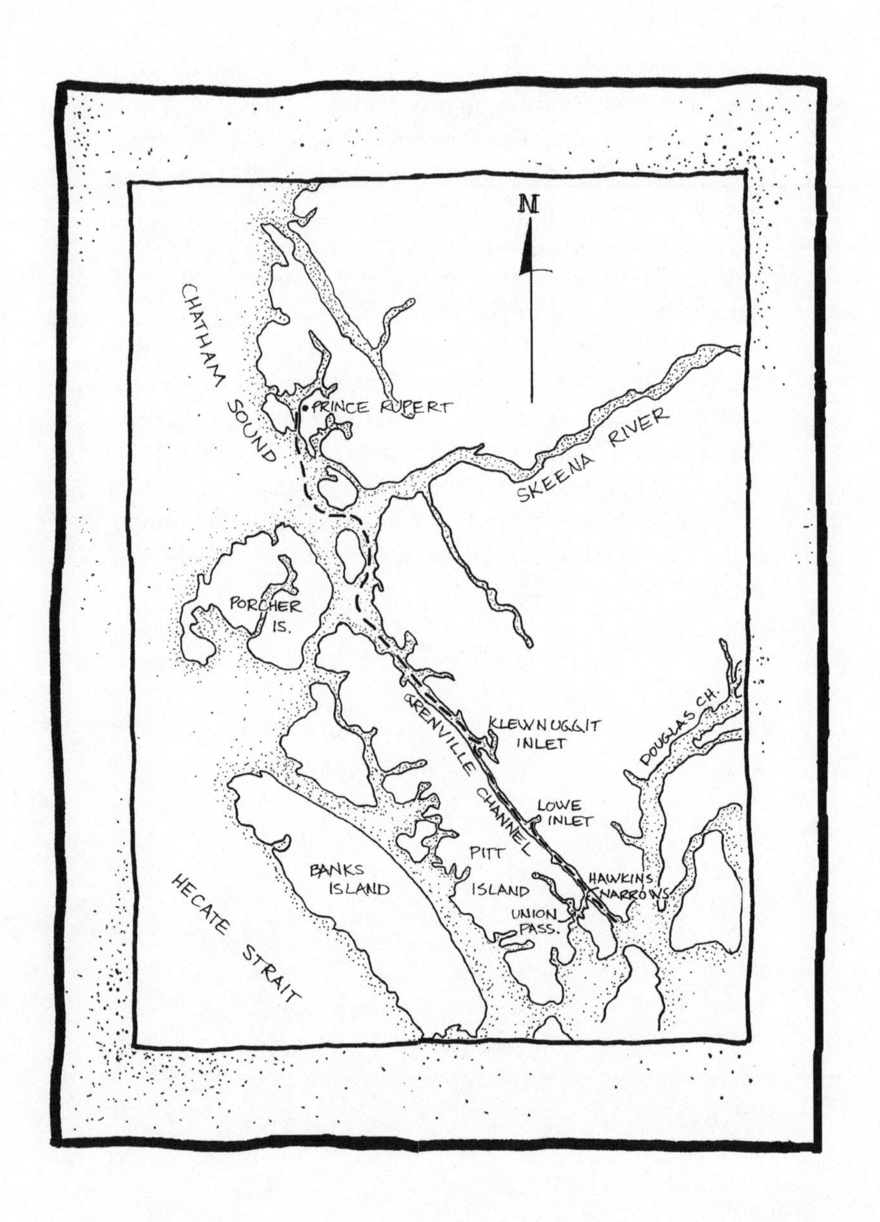
N
CHATHAM SOUND
PRINCE RUPERT
SKEENA RIVER
PORCHER IS.
GRENVILLE CHANNEL
KLEWNUGGIT INLET
DOUGLAS CH.
LOWE INLET
PITT ISLAND
BANKS ISLAND
HAWKINS NARROWS
UNION PASS.
HECATE STRAIT

Chapter Ten

Pretentious quotations being the surest road to tedium.

H. W. and F. G. Fowler,
A DICTIONARY OF
MODERN ENGLISH USAGE

DUSK IS FALLING and half a gale is blowing when *Rosebud* drops me off at the entrance to Grenville Channel. I am sorry to see her go, but after all, you can have too much of a good thing. It is time to get down to business again. The elderly kayaker has made his mark. Come to think of it, he isn't all that old. I suppose we are much of an age if anyone is counting.

It is time to think about finding somewhere to spend the night but once again I run into the problem of no bottom. The channel is narrow and the sides so precipitous they go straight up and straight down into the sea. I try both sides, no luck. The wind is strong. Against me, of course.

This is Murphy's Law or Macpherson's or somebody's. I can only push on up the channel slowly, painfully slowly, and hope for the best. The best turns out to be Hawkins Narrows, at the entrance to Union Passage where the chart tells me the current could run eight knots. Beggars can't be choosers. At least it is away from the wash of the huge cruise ships and fishing boats. It is very much a case of any port in a storm. It is getting dark and rain has started to fall.

It may seem strange that it could rain at the end of such a wonderful day of sun and wind. Well, that's the way things are on this coast. It's never boringly repetitious.

It rains hard all night. *Morag Anne* spins at her mooring but I hear no sounds of scraping on rock. All the same, I don't sleep much for the night is filled with strange groaning and moaning. I get up several times, once crawling forward on the foredeck in my pyjamas, trying to trace the source of these peculiar cries. It is black as pitch and very wet.

When dawn comes I am quite disoriented. I think at first that I must have been swept down Hawkins Channel. It takes some time to realize that everything looks different at high water and that the boat has turned completely around. My fears are groundless but there is a momentary frisson of anxiety which sets the tone of the day. The moaning and groaning I had worried about all night comes from kelp wound between the rudder and the hull, like a great, tangled ball of string stretching and relaxing with each wave. It takes more than half an hour and a lot of bad language to get free.

It is still raining hard.

In retrospect you wonder if you really enjoyed all that. How could you? I'm here to tell you that, in spite of everything and even, who knows, because of it, I wouldn't have changed places with anyone.

But it is a gloomy row up Grenville. The channel is nowhere more than a mile wide. When a cruise ship bears down on something the size of *Morag Anne* it seems very large indeed. Sometimes I feel I can reach out and touch the sides of the huge ships that slowly, very slowly and sedately slip up and down the channel. It is surprising how little wash they make. Seiners on the other hand, not all that much bigger than one of the orange lifeboats stacked like toys on the sides of the giant ships, set up a wash that makes rowing very unpleasant.

I feel sorry for the folks on the boats on such a day. They can't see to the tops of the mountainous sides of the channel; for all the view they get they could be sailing along a Dutch canal. The sea is a dull, sullen grey. A gloomy scene indeed and more so, I imagine, if you are paying the earth to see it. If you are standing on deck, hands in the pockets of your parka, woolen hat down around your ears and a drip on the end of your nose, bored out of your mind, full to the gills with breakfast and nothing to look forward to but lunch, you might well be wondering about the cost-benefit ratio. I know I would.

I am better off in *Morag Anne.*

I make for Lowe Inlet, find a snug bay and drop anchor. It is still raining but it has been a good day, one that started at four-thirty. The next inlet, Klewnuggit, is a long way up-channel. I am riding at anchor by noon and not about to apologise for stopping so early in the day. The inlet is deserted when I arrive but it doesn't stay that way long. You would have thought that every big boat between Seattle and Juneau had decided to stop by. To watch them jockeying for position is most entertaining. It is important to lie as close as you can to your neighbour, it seems. I suppose this has something to do with conviviality and the cocktail hour. The manoeuvers necessary to achieve this would tax the skill of a professional and it is clear that not many of these skippers are professionals. My sympathies go to their crews. In most cases there is one per boat and usually female. It must be a stern test of affection. The skipper, standing aft, can't hear what the crew, hanging over the bow, is calling out. The crew can't hear the skipper either. Sometimes, given the bad language and vituperation coming from the cockpit, this may not be such a bad thing.

All night long the generators roar. When one stops and sleep seems possible, another starts. I have spent better nights.

In spite of all my worry about charts and what seems at times the inordinate number I carry, I discover that I have none showing the top right hand corner of Grenville Channel. This is a real problem. The sides of the channel are very steep. Rowing or sailing blindly and hoping an anchorage will present itself has no appeal. Unless I am prepared to row all day and all night, once past Klewnuggit Inlet, a safe place to anchor is a necessity.

A couple of times a passing boat slows down to admire my pretty little boat and I call across and ask if they have the appropriate chart. Each time the navigator allows as how he has discovered the same problem. We share our chagrin but that doesn't help much.

Rowing up-channel is tedious, sea traffic is heavy in both directions and I am compelled to hug the shore. According to the tide tables, a small current should be helping me along. In my paranoid state I am convinced to the contrary and it may not all be paranoia. Tides and currents do strange things, as Belloc points out. Sometimes they have minds of their own.

Hugging the shore can double your distance. I should not let it bother me but I do. As the end approaches and I can see Prince Rupert in my mind's eye, the urge to get on as quickly as possible is too strong.

Klewnuggit Inlet is still far off when a large American yacht comes from astern, and yielding readily to temptation, I hail her and ask for a tow which is readily given.

Wanderbird of Seattle, skipper Mik Endrody and your wife Barb, I remember you tenderly for the tow and the package of fresh bread, oranges and Budweiser. You tow me to Klewnuggit, not a tremendous distance but what a lift you give my flagging spirit. I've said it before: these chance meetings are so delightful it's worth going cruising just to experience them.

In retrospect I realize I could have reached Prince Rupert without the next tow that I accept. Hindsight is such a useful tool. Like the Amex Card, I suppose you should never leave home without it. But that's all very well and good. What you really need is foresight and I haven't yet found that tool. Especially not at sea. The future is a guess and the smaller your boat the greater the guess and the more dire the consequences if you guess wrong.

I can't raise Prince Rupert Coast Guard on my tiny receiver. There is no way to be sure what next day's weather will be like. Oh, you can look at the sky when you turn in for the night. Sniff the wind if you like, but in the final analysis, it's still a guess. I am snug as you like in my little bay in Klewnuggit but I must admit that with the end of the adventure so tantalizingly close, my one great ambition is to finish it in style. In style if possible, but if not, then at least in safety. Too anxious? I freely admit it.

I don't sleep well.

The next morning is clearly the start of what is going to be a dirty day. The clouds are down to waterline, the sea choppy and confused and there is a breeze from the northwest that promises to become worse.

The sensible course would be to stay in Klewnuggit. First light is somewhere about four a.m. and it is a miserable sight.

The mist of early morning gets thicker, and the sea rougher as I enter the main channel. The tidal current is in my favour, which is why I set off so early. I try to make for the starboard shore but it is tough going. I move ever so slowly up the channel crabwise. Retreat is still possible and I think seriously about it when I spot a single light moving very slowly astern.

Gradually, out of the murky, misty morning haze I make out the white hull of a lovely yacht under power, a light at her masthead. As she passes across my bow, close enough to discern the oilskinned helmsman, I make my decision. Right or wrong, think I, I'm going to ask for help.

At my signal, *Nonpareil* slows and comes towards *Morag Anne* and thus I encounter John and Noel Myers from Portland, Oregon, who take my line. For the first half hour I huddle down in my foul-weather gear, comfortable enough in the sternsheets of *Morag Anne.* Wind blows the clouds away and raises an unpleasant sea. *Nonpareil* slows, John Myers leans over the transom.

"You had best come aboard. We have just heard a forecast. It's dirty weather coming. Northwest winds gusting to gale force. If we let you go here I don't know where you'll find any shelter. Unless you're very determined to go it alone, we'll tow you to Rupert."

Decisions, decisions. What to do? He is right, of course, and there is also the matter of the missing chart of the top end of the channel. On the other hand, this is the end of the voyage. Can I sneak into Rupert, tail between my legs, under tow? What is the alternative?

Prince Rupert is a busy port. Ferries come from both the south and north not to mention the heavy deep-sea traffic in grain and coal. Then there is the Skeena River outflow current and a maze of islands to contend with. In good weather all these hazards could probably be handled.

This is not good weather. It is going to get worse. I go aboard *Nonpareil* and make one of the best decisions of my life.

The wind increases. Soon the skipper decides conditions are bad enough to rule out an attempt to reach Rupert. We head for shelter behind the Micmicking Islands in Bloxham Passage where we spend a night at anchor in rough seas, listening to wind howling in the shrouds, surf breaking on the rocky shore of the closest island and the flapping of *Nonpareil's* canvas dodger.

John and Noel are superb hosts. They feed me royally: fresh crabmeat, homemade bread, California wines and yarns galore. Nothing will do but that I sleep in the cockpit. They won't countenance my going back to *Morag Anne* to put up the tent, dry the deck and unroll my sleeping bag. And so it is, anticlimax or no, that I spend the last night of the adventure not in *Morag Anne,* but on board *Nonpareil* in luxury and comfort.

I don't sleep a wink.

Morag Anne is determined to move up from astern, continually butting the beautiful white hull of *Nonpareil,* and I in pyjamas, equally determinedly fending her off throughout the night. Most unusual behaviour for a small boat on a painter. I can only blame the very rough, confused sea.

Morning brings breakfast, calmer weather, heavy rain and an oily swell. The sight of the high, bluff sides of an empty grain ship nosing in from the Pacific through the rain decides me against making my way into Prince Rupert harbour under oar power alone. *Nonpareil* tows me the rest of the way and my entry is appropriately anticlimactic.

John needs fuel to continue the voyage to Juneau so we make for the gas company wharves. Cast loose, I proceed alongside one of them while John maneuvers the tricky approach in *Nonpareil.* A large zodiac inflatable with an orange-dressed Coast Guard crew comes close.

"Can you direct me to the nearest telephone?" I ask.

They don't appear very interested.

"Look," I say, "I've just come in after rowing up from Port Hardy. I want to phone my wife."

"Port Hardy, eh? Don't bullshit us." They put their motor to full throttle and roar off.

Envoi.

KENNETH MACRAE LEIGHTON DIED
JUNE 19, 1998 OF COMPLICATIONS
RELATED TO HEPATITIS C.

About the book

This book was produced by Group of One Design, Telkwa, British Columbia. It was printed and bound by Friesens of Altona, Manitoba.

The text is set in Korinna regular. The original drawings for this typeface were executed at H. Berthold AG of Berlin in 1904. Brought out of obscurity by its vigourous and rather individual character, in 1974 ITC Korinna was developed into a family of four weights by Benguiat and staff at Photo-Lettering Inc. of New York.

The illustrations are done in a *sgraffito* technique on either clayboard or scratchboard.